The Life & Art of the
North American
INDIAN

The Life & Art of the
North American INDIAN

John Anson Warner

Associate Professor, Department of Sociology,
University of Regina, Canada

Crescent Books
New York

PEHRISKA-RUHPA

FOR MY FATHER, MOTHER AND SISTER

Published by
The Hamlyn Publishing Group Limited
London · New York · Sydney · Toronto
Astronaut House, Feltham, Middlesex, England

© Copyright The Hamlyn Publishing Group Limited 1975

Distributed in the USA by Crescent Books

Library of Congress
Catalog Card No: 74-19934

ISBN 0-517-131277

Phototypeset in England by
Filmtype Services Limited, Scarborough
Color reproduction by
Colour Workshop Limited, Hertford, England

Printed in Spain by
Printer Industria Gráfica sa, Tuset 19
Barcelona, San Vicente dels Horts 1975
Depósito Legal B. 38059-1974
Mohn-Gordon Limited, London

endpapers: Hupa trout trap. Photograph by Edward S. Curtis
half title: The three chiefs, Piegan. Photograph by Edward S. Curtis
contents page: A feast day at Acoma. Photograph by Edward S. Curtis

Contents

Introduction

It was not so many years ago that North American Indian arts and crafts were classified in the category of souvenirs or trinkets that one might bring home as a remembrance of a visit to some exotic region within the continent. At best, the historic and prehistoric relics of a once great people were housed in museums of natural history as examples of 'primitive art.' Within recent years the situation has changed quickly and dramatically. Art lovers and connoisseurs from all over the world are coming to recognize the arts of the North American Indian as one of the truly distinguished artistic traditions of mankind. As with the case of African and Oceanic art, collections of North American material are leaving the cloistered halls of natural history museums and finding their way into art museums and galleries in the major cultural capitals of the world. Clearly, this is an art form whose time has come.

The question that might be asked is why? Why has an art form, so long ignored by major arbiters of artistic taste in the Western world, now come to such popularity and wide-ranging acceptance? Part of the answer may lie simply in the fact that it was inevitable that sooner or later a bored and jaded public would discover a native art which possesses generous amounts of vitality and originality. Certainly it was clear that if African and Oceanic art could be appreciated for their intrinsic excellence, the discovery of North American Indian arts and crafts would not be long in coming. It was simply unreasonable that such a tradition could be overlooked indefinitely. However, perhaps there is a more profound answer awaiting us.

We are living in a time when, to borrow a phrase and book title of Sigmund Freud's, civilization and its discontents are becoming painfully evident to us all. Our machine age technology with its private greed, ecologically disastrous policies, crass materialism, human alienation, incessant strife and conflict, and the portent of man's destroying himself by his own recklessness, is taking its toll in terms of our confidence and optimism about life. We are no longer so sure about the inevitability of progress in our modern social life and few, it seems, would care to argue the proposition that this is 'the best of all possible worlds.' Our existence as men is rife with violence, unhappiness, loneliness, and insecurity. We search for meaning and solace in human life and all too often what we find turns to ashes in our hands. The mass media bombard us with instantaneous reportage of all that is wrong with our world and this, more often than not, serves to reinforce our sense of frustration and fear.

When we turn to our popular culture—which includes the arts—for diversion and meaning, we are confused, oftentimes, by the welter of contradictory impressions. We are trivialized and mesmerized by the pap that is purveyed on the television and radio, and in newspapers and magazines. We take away from our experience with these forms of entertainment a sense of having spent time but not having been taught anything or having been ennobled. We learn without understanding and visualize without seeing. Popular culture often strikes us as simply a mode of whiling away time instead of an experience that interprets and explains our lives. We are told that casual sex and pornography are 'art forms' of our time, and we know better. The television batters us senseless with lobotomizing trivia, gladiatorial extravaganzas that reduce us to the role of passive observers, and kiddy shows that urge our children to grow up to be consumers and materialists along with the best of them. The highbrow art found in the official art museums, concert halls, and legitimate theaters often strikes the common person as something to which he cannot aspire. The plastic arts are too abstract and 'weird' for his taste, the music too esoteric and complicated, and the plays are for those with doctorates and/or eccentric tastes in philosophy. All this describes a widening gulf between the mass public with the vulgarization of its tastes and the rarefied atmosphere of the intellectual elite who cultivate their sensitive tastes with specialized diversions. Placed within the context of a society where there is obvious exploitation, crude violence, and a strong sense of anxiety, our cultural milieu is not a happy one.

Moreover, many of our young and those who consider themselves to be intellectuals perceive these troubles and seek to understand them. Many, particularly in recent years, go so far as to seek out modes of consciousness or states of awareness that are different from ordinary reality. The tremendous fame and popularity of anthropologist Carlos Castaneda, author of *The Teachings of Don Juan: A Yaqui Way of Knowledge*, *A Separate Reality: Further Conversations with Don Juan*, and *Journey to Ixtlan: The Lessons of Don Juan*, give ample testimony on how the movement in search of 'separate realities' has grown in recent years. Many in our post-industrial societies (the term used by Jacques Ellul and Herbert Marcuse) are seeking alternatives because 'ordinary reality' seems so unpleasant. For a few this search for something else, or something more than is present in the status quo society, suggests militant political activity of a Marxist nature. For others, this search causes them to explore other cultures with their different beliefs, social structures, and behaviour patterns. Among those cultures which are sometimes sought out are those of the North American Indian.

*1. Nootka method of spearing. The Nootka use a double-
headed harpoon for spearing seals, porpoises and salmon.
Photograph by Edward S. Curtis*

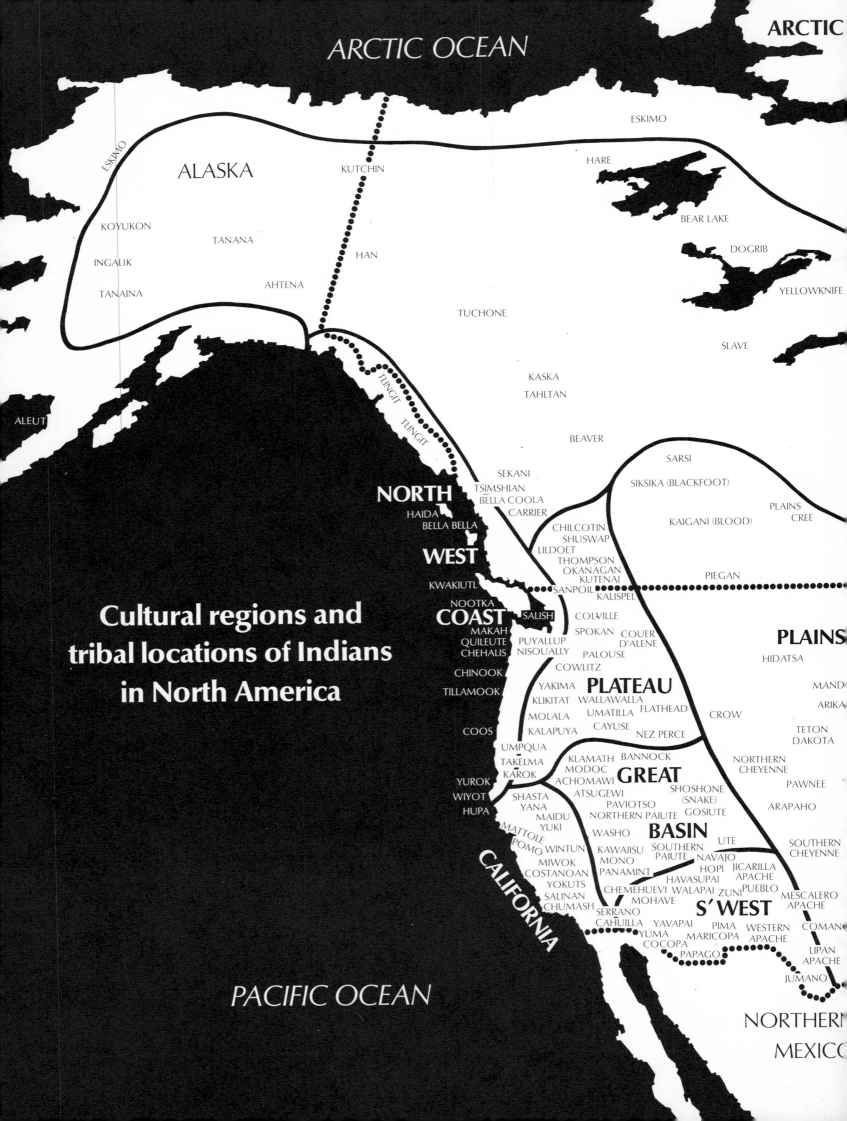

ESKIMO

ESKIMO

ATLANTIC
OCEAN

ESKIMO

HUDSON BAY

CHIPEWYAN

SUBARCTIC

CREE

CREE

NASKAPI
MONTAGNAIS

BEOTHUK

INA
NIBOINE

OJIBWAY (CHIPPEWA)

HURON

MICMAC
MALECITE
ABNAKI
PASSAMAQUODDY

OTTAWA

OJIBWAY

MENOMINEE

TIONANTATI

HURON

MAHICAN

PENOBSCOT
PENNACOOK

SAUX
& FOX

WINNEBAGO

POTOWATOMI

NEUTRAL

MOHAWK
ONEIDA
ONONDAGA
CAYUGA
SENECA

MASSACHUSET
WAMPANOAG
NIANTIC
NAUSET

SANTEE
DAKOTA

NKTON
KOTA

KICKAPOO

NIPMUC

NARRAGANSET

PONCA

IOWA

KASKASKIA

EASTERN
WOODLAND

SUSQUEHANNA
(CONESTOGA)

PEQUOT
MOHEGAN
WAPPINGER

ILLINOIS

OMAHA
OTO

KANSA

MISSOURI

PEORIA

MIAMI
WEA
PIANKASHAW

PAMUNKEY

DELAWARE (LENNI LANAPE)
NANTICOKE

CHICKAHOMINY

OSAGE

WA

SHAWNEE

MATTAPONY
TUTELO

POWHATAN

PAMLICO

OWA
ACHE

TAWAKONI

QUAPAW

CHEROKEE
YUCHI
TUSKEGEE

NOTTAWAY
TUSCARORA
CATAWBA

CHICKASAW

CHITA

S'EAST

CREEK

ATLANTIC OCEAN

CADDO

CHOCTAW

YAMASEE

KICHAI
WACO
TONKAWA

TUNICA
NATCHEZ
HOUMA

ALABAMA

HITCHITI

APALACHEE

GUALE

TIMUCUA

ATAKAPA

CHITIMACHA

BILOXI

MOBILE

GULF OF
MEXICO

SEMINOLE

CALUSA

In an age where many are tired of the materialism and ecologically destructive facets of modern society, the cultures of the North American Indian seem to offer a refreshing alternative to these modes of life. There has been a renewed interest in the Indian whose outlook on life, particularly before he came under the subjugation of white authority, spoke of reverence for nature and a conviction that man must live in harmony with all the elements of natural existence. The Indian was an ecologist by cultural conviction, and his whole way of life gave testimony to the principle that every single thing on the earth is a part of the whole and that whole is a harmony in the universe. Possessing a profoundly spiritual outlook on life, one that often went into the mystical realm, the Indian felt that there is an intimate relationship (or brotherhood) between all things, animate and inanimate. A man is related to all existence as it, in turn, is related to him. We are diminished by the subtraction from that existence and we are made more whole by the growth of that existence. Gayle High Pines expressed it well when she said:

'We are the whole Earth, spiritually plugged into her every process—we hear her every cry. If we lose our ability to hear, we cannot flow in harmony with her, and we will vanish with the invaders when she resolves this dissonance with a great convulsive shudder.'
(*Akwesasne Notes*, Rooseveltown, New York, Oct. 1973.)

The sense, then, that a great and uniting spirit pervades everything in nature, and that this unity has a certain nobility in its wholeness, is a hallmark of Indian consciousness. It is a conception that informs us that there is more to things than we can perceive by merely regarding their outward forms and appearance. Indeed, the whole is very much something more than what it appears to be merely to our gross senses. There reposes in existence an essence which can be discerned by those who have the will to understand, in the fullest sense of that word.

As the Indian tends to look at it, if everything is a part of the whole then all the units of existence are equal with each other. I, as a man, have my place in the universe but that place is not better than nor worse than the places of all other entities. The trees, stones, animals, soil, sky, sun, and moon are, along with man, cohabitants of the universe and each is a precious unit within the whole. His is an imagination that believes that time and space are elements of an eternal whole and harmony is the law of such a universe.

One of the leading experts in the field of Indian culture and how the consciousness of these people might be structured is Frank Waters. He has written a number of sensitive accounts about the Indian outlook, including *Masked Gods*, *The Book of Hopi*, and *Pumpkin Seed Point*. In his first major work, *The Man Who Killed the Deer*, written in 1942, Waters authored a fictional account of how one Indian man from Taos Pueblo in New Mexico came face to face with the outlook of his people. It is the story of Martiniano who was born in the old Pueblo but who returned home after an extended period of time in the white man's world. Imbued with many of the white man's values, Martiniano had difficulty reorienting himself to the more sensitive and delicately balanced Puebloan view of the world. More specifically, Martiniano got himself into trouble by thoughtlessly and heedlessly killing a deer in a manner that contravened tribal custom. In rebuking him for his improper behaviour, the head priest of the Pueblo (called a *Cacique*) had the following to say to Martiniano. In his address, the *Cacique* summarizes much of the profound philosophy that characterizes what we have termed the Indian outlook on life:

'There is no such thing as a simple thing. One drops a pebble into a pool, but the ripples travel far. One picks up a little stone in the mountains, one of the little stones called Lagrimas de Cristo—and look! It is shaped like a star; the sloping mountain is full of stars as the sloping sky. Or take a kernel of corn. Plant it in Our Mother Earth with the sweat of your body, with what you know of the times and seasons, with your proper prayers. And with your strength and manhood Our Father Sun multiplies and gives it back into your flesh. What then is this kernel of corn? It is not a simple thing.

'Nothing is simple and alone. We are not separate and alone. The breathing mountains, the living stones, each blade of grass, the clouds, the rain, each star, the beasts, the birds and the invisible spirits of the air—we are all one, indivisible. Nothing that any of us does but affects us all.

'So I would have you look upon this thing not as a separate simple thing, but as a stone which is a star in the firmament of earth, as a ripple in a pool, as a kernel of corn. I would have you consider how it fits into the pattern of the whole. How far its influence may spread. What it may grow into . . .

'So there is something else to consider. The deer. It is dead. In the old days we all remember, we did not go out on a hunt lightly. We said to the deer we were going to kill, "We know your life is as precious as ours. We know that we are both children of the same Great True Ones. We know that we are all one life on the same Mother Earth, beneath the same plains of the sky. But we also know that one life must sometimes give way to another so that the one great life of all may continue unbroken. So we ask your permission, we obtain your consent to this killing."

'Ceremonially we said this, and we sprinkled meal and corn pollen to Our Father Sun. And when we killed the deer we laid his head toward the East, and sprinkled him with meal and pollen. And we dropped drops of his blood and bits of his flesh on the ground for Our Mother Earth. It was proper so. For then when we too built its flesh into our flesh, when we walked in the moccasins of its skin, when we danced in its robe and antlers, we knew that the life of the deer was continued in our life, as it in turn was continued in the one life all around us, below us and above us.

'We knew the deer knew this and was satisfied.

'But this deer's permission was not obtained. What have we done to this deer, our brother? What have we done to ourselves? For we are all bound together, and our touch upon one travels through all to return to us again. Let us not forget the deer.'

And so, in the incomparable prose of Frank Waters which seems to capture the spirit of Indian thought so well, we gain an appreciation of how the Indian is aware of and responds to his world.

The art of these people, which is a material expression of their cultural outlook, portrays such a consciousness in a myriad of ways. It is a cultural view such as this which attracts so many who are tired and discouraged by the prospect of contemporary North American (and European) civilization. Frank Waters' books have become best sellers in the United States, and whole communities of young people search in the wisdom of the Indian viewpoint for a new interpretation of life and the meaning of existence. Their resulting affection for North American Indian art is one reflection of a resurgence in Indian culture as a whole.

This is not to suggest that explicit cultural alienation is the only reason for the growth in the popularity of this art, however. It is but one factor, albeit a factor of considerable importance. On a less exalted ideological plane, many are attracted to these native arts and crafts by a sense of romanticism and nostalgia for the past. In any age where contemporary life seems to offer many problems and dilemmas, whole categories of people respond not with an explicit denial of the ongoing cultural values but seek out, instead, a more gentle and romantic version of life. This diversion from the harsh realities of everyday life can take many forms. One of the forms it might embrace is an affection for the culture of another people who have not and do not seem to be placed in the same predicament as oneself. The life of these people is interpreted as less painful and more simple than our own. Also, the gratifications of life within such a culture are emphasized and brought out in bold relief. By a kind of vicarious association with such a culture, people find themselves relieved of some of the psychological burdens of everyday life in the real world and derive considerable gratification from such an identification. To see and enjoy the art of such a different people is intrinsically rewarding, and their distinctive imagination is appreciated in terms of the characteristic cultural forms which it represents. Thus, for many in the workaday world of modern civilization, it is a pleasing experience to be able to appreciate the art of a people who seem to have lived in a less demanding world; or so we are prone to think.

Apart from the cultural alienation of some intellectuals and the particular brand of romanticism which is common in the Western world, a final factor of importance in accounting for the surge of interest in Indian art can be found in the current controversies surrounding the role of the Indian in the history of North America. There has been a considerabe amount of re-examination of late with regard to the record of white treatment of native peoples in New World history. The publication and subsequent commercial success of Dee Brown's *Bury My Heart at Wounded Knee* is symbolic of the reassessment now taking place regarding the justice of the arrangements worked out between the white man and the Indian. The brutality of white policies and the utter ruthlessness with which they were executed are now emerging into the light of popular scholarship. The cynicism, lies, cheating, racism, and violence which characterized white behaviour in the march across the continent are coming to be understood as the common traits of the relationship between the two races. As this history is revealed, compassion and understanding for the travail of the North American Indian grows.

This situation is further highlighted by the efforts of new Indian leaders in our time to redress some of the old wrongs and gain a better place for Indian peoples in North American society. The world is reminded of the terrible wrongs perpetrated against the Indian people in the past when modern leaders protest the inheritance of those wrongs today. The fearful massacre of the Sioux at Wounded Knee, South Dakota, in 1890, is brought to public awareness by the events at Wounded Knee in 1973. The purpose of such events is to show that the Sioux people are still suffering grievously from the effects of such subjugation when it was effected in 1890. From around 1890 on, the North American Indians virtually ceased to be a people in the society of the New World. Ignored and left alone to cope with their poverty and misery, the Indians languished from official neglect and indifference for over half a century. What little was done for them by the governments of the United States and Canada barely served to keep them alive. The bitter heritage of this state of affairs is now being made known throughout the world as it has stirred a guilty conscience within many white people.

For too long the Indians have had to say, 'For us only the past lives.' The present and the future have held little or no promise for the Indian and this has taken a tremendous toll on the quality of his life. To rectify this state of affairs the past must be made known and the present situation must be changed.

In any case, this reinterpretation of American and Canadian history and the efforts of Indian leadership from this generation to redress a sorry state of affairs have stirred the imagination of many. In the light of such activity, the old racist attitudes about the inferiority of Indian culture are being re-examined and set aside. Indian culture and history are being reassessed in order to uncover the truth about a very great people. As a part of that process, it is inevitable that their art should be rediscovered.

The reaffimation of the greatness of North American Indian art did not come all at once. On the contrary, it has been a matter which has been part of the total process of the recovery of the Indian as a viable member of the national communities of the United States

6. *Beaded bag. Cree, Canada. Museum of the American Indian, Heye Foundation, New York*

opposite 7. **Kee-a-kee-ka-sa-coo-way** *(The man who gives the war whoop), by Paul Kane. 1848. Oil, 30 × 25 in. Head chief of the Crees with his pipe stem. Royal Ontario Museum, Toronto*

and Canada and therefore it has been a long and arduous climb upwards. As we have just pointed out, the Indian was shunted aside and ignored for a very long period of time in North America.

In terms of the emergence of the arts and crafts as a cultural heritage worthy of respect, nothing systematic was done in the United States until the administration of Franklin D. Roosevelt in the 1930s. Under the inspired and gifted leadership of John Collier, the Bureau of Indian Affairs in the FDR administration began the difficult reorientation of policy. In particular, the government began to change its attitude that Indians should stop being Indians just as soon as possible and completely disappear into the majority white culture. Although such a policy was bitterly opposed by the Indians throughout the United States, their resistance was largely of a passive nature. Collier's greater sympathy for the need of Indian people to retain their identity and not to be submerged in the 'melting pot' of America found a ready response amongst many on the US reservations. His establishment of policies for self-government in the Indian Reorganization Act was hailed by many as a first step in the process of restoring faith to a people whose will had been almost shattered in the previous half century. For Indians who had to cope with the iron governance of an Indian Agent appointed from Washington, and who had to survive the ever-present ridiculing of their traditions by a whole bevy of missionaries and teachers, the Collier administration's fresh policies helped generate new hope.

In the cultural realm, Collier initiated several new policies that indicated respect for the Indian way. He began the process of removing the emphasis placed on off-reservation education in boarding schools for primary and secondary grades. Instead, more and more on-reservation day schools were established so the Indian child could continue to live at home while receiving the requisite schooling. In terms of arts and crafts, Collier helped to establish an Arts and Crafts Board in the Department of the Interior so that the finest in traditional and contemporary arts could be encouraged with government support. This Board still exists today. It is active in the promotion and support of craftsmen and artists in sponsoring exhibitions, overseeing the Institute for American Indian Arts in Santa Fe, New Mexico, funding workshops and demonstration centers for aspiring artisans, and maintaining a program of certification for authentic arts and crafts.

Coterminous with these developments was the work of citizen groups in the United States. Many concerned people, recognizing the severe plight of the American Indian on his reservations, joined together in voluntary organizations to try to do something about this state of affairs. One of the most important of these groups was the Eastern Association on Indian Affairs which was led by the distinguished champion of Indian culture, Oliver La Farge. The Association was extremely active in the 1920s with regard to the investigation of violation of Indian civil rights and the blatant conditions of poverty and disease on various reservations. When La Farge joined the Association in 1930, he was much encouraged by the prospect of a change in governmental policy towards Indians. As a result of a Brookings Institute study written in 1928 by Lewis Meriam and associates, entitled *The Problem of Indian Administration*, the Republican administration of Herbert Hoover came to recognize the seriousness of the situation. In 1929 Hoover appointed Charles J. Rhoads Commissioner of Indian Affairs, and Rhoads began the slow process of redressing the grievances of a people accumulated over half a century; a process, as we have said, to be accelerated by Collier in the FDR years.

Although hampered by a lack of funds and not a great deal of power, Rhoads did what he could to help ameliorate conditions amongst American Indians. Rhoads was a special enthusiast of arts and crafts, and it was during his tenure that an event of special importance occurred with respect to this subject. Under Oliver La Farge's direction, the Eastern Association on Indian Affairs sponsored an important exhibition of Indian arts and crafts in New York City. The Exposition of Indian Tribal Arts opened in New York City in December of 1931 at the Grand Central Art Gallery and was an immediate success. For the first time in the United States a major exhibition of native arts and crafts from all over the country was gathered together and presented to a cosmopolitan public. While there had been isolated and local efforts to present Indian art in a more favorable light, this was the first time attention had been drawn to Indian work on a large scale. Its success was a harbinger of things to come.

La Farge and John Sloan, a painter, collaborated on the production of an illustrated catalogue of the Exposition's material. Entitled *Introduction to American Indian Art*, it served not only as a souvenir of a memorable exhibition but also as a comprehensive and popular introduction to the entire subject. It was the first effort of its sort and it remains as a historic landmark in the emergence of literature on Indian arts and crafts.

As we have pointed out earlier, Collier's administration in the remainder of the 1930s developed and amplified upon such beginnings in more important and tangible ways. Some ten years after the Exposition of Indian Tribal Arts there was another major exhibition in New York City which called attention to the growing importance of American Indian culture. No greater champion of Indian art can be found than the late René d'Harnoncourt whose position in New York's Museum of Modern Art enabled him to promote it whenever the opportunity availed itself. In 1941 an exhibition entitled 'Indian Art of the United States' was organized, and d'Harnoncourt collaborated with Frederic H. Douglas in order to produce an illustrated book of the same title. It was the second major Indian cultural exhibition in New York City and out of it emerged a second introductory volume on the subject which was to endure as a seminal work.

Since that time there have been many exhibitions and shows devoted to one or other aspect of native arts and crafts. Most recently, the Whitney Museum of American Art devoted its whole facilities from 16th November 1971 to 9th January 1972 in order to hold a comprehensive exhibition entitled '200 Years of North American Indian Art'. *Time* magazine hailed it as not only a critical and artistic success but as a symbol that Indian art had truly come of age in arts circles. Moreover, the Whitney Museum's show served to point out that Indian art is no longer something to be tucked away in natural history museums or denigrated with the label of 'primitive art.' It is, indeed, a highly sophisticated art form which is worthy of study and appreciation by cosmopolitan art critics anywhere in the world.

Thus three New York shows have highlighted the emergence of Indian arts and crafts out of the shadows of racism and obscurity into the sunlight of acclaim and recognition: the Exposition of Indian Tribal Arts in 1931, the Indian Art of the United States Exhibition in 1941, and 200 Years of North American Indian Art in 1971. Norman Feder's very handsome catalogue of the last named exhibition brings our awareness of such success to an explicit point.

Any inspection of North American Indian art, whether at a museum exhibition or from illustrations such as those in this book, will reveal that there are certain general themes in this material. While generalizations must always be tentative and subject to revision, it is clear that certain characteristics do present themselves when Indian art is comprehended as a whole. Although numerous exceptions to any assertion will be manifest, it is nonetheless true that a number of high level generalizations can be put forth.

One trait of Indian art which can be discerned is its manifest tendency towards abstraction. This tendency can be particularly well shown when pre-white-contact and post-white-contact art forms are compared. Before the coming of the white man in North America, Indian arts and crafts tended to be distinctly non-representational in character. That is to say, Indian art very rarely attempted to portray objects as they appear in a commonsense visual world. Whereas European art, particularly in the 16th, 17th and 18th centuries, embraced an approach exhibiting fidelity to natural appearances in the real world, Indian art almost never made that kind of effort. European painting, for instance, emphasized realism of a definite sort and the canvases of its masters tended to show the world as it actually appears to the eye. The Enlightenment, Capitalism, and Protestantism combined together to induce art forms which were narrative and realist, often in the very best sense of that word. This is not to argue that even realism is not interpretable but to suggest that when a tree is painted it tends to look like a tree, even as a photograph would have it.

Pre-contact Indian art, on the other hand, almost never sought such scientific fidelity. Instead, the Indian imagination sought to interpret a subject so that its 'essence' rather than its mere 'appearance' would emerge in the work of art. In other words, the Indian artist endeavored to capture the whole truth of a subject rather than only what we can see. It is a subjective art as opposed to an objective art. For the Indian, there is something more in nature than just what we can visually perceive; there are whole dimensions of existence which are not amenable to simple narration. Our sense perceptions can only give us a part of the truth for the whole truth is something much more. Whenever a native artist addressed the truth of a natural subject, he was more interested in capturing the true form and essence of that subject than he was in realistically portraying it as the eye would capture it. Therefore, what the imagination of the Indian demanded was an approximation of the whole essence rather than a particularization of the visual appearance.

If this sounds mystical or spiritual, such a portrayal would not be far from the truth, for Indian conscious-

ness was of that sort. As we suggested earlier, the Indian had a very special conception about himself and his relationship to nature and the universe. For him, the categories which we of the rational Western world have created possess little value. On the contrary, in the Indian's world of perception, as it was for G. W. F. Hegel, 'the truth is the whole.' That whole is the oneness and unity of the universe in which all units of the whole are organically related to each other. The Indian loved the land, the animals, the sky, the trees, and all of creation as he loved his human brethren. What he sought, in terms of understanding, was to comprehend the essential truth of the whole as it was manifested in the various parts of existence. Thus, mere appearance could be quite deceiving. Truth, in sum, transcends sense perception. Indian artists in the various cultures often went to considerable effort in order to realize this realm of awareness.

Insofar as Indian imagination attempted to go beyond the material base of objects, the conception of a subject in their art form is often perplexing to the Western viewer. Often he will see something and respond to it with intuitive pleasure but be unfamiliar with the identity of the subject being portrayed. Such instances might abound in this book. What will help us in our appreciation of Indian art is an awareness of this principle of abstraction.

In addition to abstraction, symbolism is another dominant motif of Indian arts and crafts. Symbolism is where a figure, character, or mark serves to represent the object in question. Very often within a tribal art tradition, it would be common to portray a mountain or rainbow or abode with some conventionalized symbol. This symbol, when seen, would be understood by all within the culture as representing some object or idea common to the life of the people.

Sometimes symbols or abstractions did not have a life of only temporary duration. Oftentimes these abstractions and symbols would be utilized characteristically and conventionally over a long period of time. When this was true, we can speak of Indian art as tending to become stylized. That is, the art would contain certain abstractions and symbols which might be used time and again in order to suggest readily to any viewer within the culture a whole complex of meanings. Change, therefore, would usually come as the result of slow innovation and evolution in Indian art. While sudden or revolutionary changes were possible, these would usually take place in the manner of some wholly new form of art appearing to take its place alongside more traditional forms. We are not here referring to technological change (like that brought by the introduction of new tools by white traders) but to whole new art forms not previously made. Thus, stylization in Indian art tends to suggest a certain conservatism in a particular artistic tradition.

A final salient characteristic of Indian art, one which should require little elaboration, reposes in the fact that there was no 'art for art's sake' as we would know it. While that term is not entirely a felicitous one, it does serve to suggest the principle that Indian art was utilitarian until very recent times. What this means is that art tended to be something one integrated into the useful objects of everyday and ceremonial life. Indeed, we might say that Indians were not aware of art as something separate from the things of real life.

below 8. Maidenhair fern basket and cover. Yellow and black design on buff base. Height 5·5 in. Karok, California. Museum of the American Indian, Heye Foundation, New York

opposite 9. Frontlet headdress, carved of cedar and inlaid with abalone shell. About 1875. Niska, British Columbia, Canada. Museum of the American Indian, Heye Foundation, New York

Art was simply the making beautiful of those objects one required in order to carry out a life dictated by the relevant culture. Beauty and utility were synonymous terms of reference in Indian culture. Art, as a category of expression different from the expression of things in everyday life, was an unknown phenomenon. While we in the Western world are all too often familiar with the distinction of art as something beautiful and special in life, set apart from the ugly and mundane things of our functional existence, the Indian conceived the two as one.

Therefore, Indian art (especially in pre-contact times) is something we see in relationship to the tools, utensils, clothing, habitats, and ceremonial paraphernalia of the life to which it was connected. The intrinsic connection between art and function witnessed in Indian life is something which we in the Western world are seeking to recover with great pain. The notion that something we use in common life can be a work of art as well is a principle well known to Indian peoples in North America.

While on the subject of the characteristics of Indian art, however, it should be emphasized that native culture was never a static or unchanging phenomenon. Even before the epoch of white contact, Indian peoples were constantly exchanging ideas and being influenced by new developments in North America. Since we know that the New World was not settled all at once in a single wave of immigration, we are aware of the fact that wave after wave of different peoples entered the new continent bringing with them diverse cultures. These differing waves of culture must have swept upon earlier inhabitants causing innovations and hybrid cultural forms to develop. This process was an ongoing one even at the time of white discovery in 1492. As we shall discern in our examination of prehistoric Indian cultures, there was considerable variability from region to region and dynamic development within the regions themselves.

It is well nigh impossible to freeze Indian culture at any special stage and say that here, and here only, is the real or genuine form of indigenous Indian arts. To attempt to decide arbitrarily that one period in an Indian culture is witness to more 'authentic' arts and crafts than some other period is a futile exercise. The process of development in Indian arts was always dynamic, with many influences outside a specific culture operating for any number of reasons. It is just not possible for us to select a special stage or time phase of any culture and decide that here the arts and crafts are 'pure' or 'pristine' or 'uncontaminated by outside influence.' Indian cultures have been, preeminently, cultures of adaptation to outside influences. In speaking of Indian art as a whole or with respect to an individual culture in time, we will always be speaking of a development which is heterodox and varied in style.

This problem occurs most frequently when some critics view the development of Indian art in a post-white-contact period. Some will argue that the white man's technology and ideas, both of which were adopted by tribes in varying degrees at different times, corrupted and spoiled an indigenous development. Moreover, many feel that there is something inferior or undesirable about Indian arts and crafts which have been touched by white influence in some way, direct or indirect. What most of these critics are unable to agree about, of course, is what development at what time in what culture can be said to be the 'turning point' in the degeneracy of arts amongst those people. There is no agreement, most likely, because such decisions are wholly arbitrary. More importantly, such decisions usually involve the personal value judgments of the critic in question and therefore are confined to his paradigmatic framework.

Our position in this volume will be that Indian arts and crafts have had a continuous existence from prehistoric times to the present day. While there was a hiatus in arts and crafts production from around 1890 to 1930 (which was both quantitative and qualitative in nature), the continuity of this tradition is remarkable. There has been, to be sure, great change within this continuity and nothing is the same as it once was; but a tradition is there and it is truly resilient.

To be more specific about the advent of the white man in terms of native arts, it can be said that the two primary inputs initially were in technology and ideas. All over North America the fur trade had a profound effect on the life of the tribes involved. In exchange for their furs, Indians were provided with a whole range of tools and consumer goods which were unknown to them previously. At least in the earlier stages of white contact (before white presence in their lands became a fact of overwhelming importance) the Indians greatly benefited from the introduction to white man's commodities. They gained a technology that more often than not enabled them to realize important potentials within their own cultures. With the new tools and goods, they could do things within their own cultural matrix which might have been impossible, or at least improbable on an important scale, before the advent of such innovations. We are quite sure, for instance, that the Northwest Coast totemic culture could not have developed in full until and unless the fur trade came to their Pacific shores with the tools for elaborate woodcarving. Without the iron and steel tools provided by white traders the Haida or Kwakiutl could never have developed their art to such an elaborate degree.

While we should never forget the fact that the white man also brought with him dreaded diseases (like smallpox and measles), to which the Indians had no natural immunity, and the plague of alcohol, it is nevertheless true that his technology and ideas did provoke a cultural development amongst the Indians who came in contact with the fur trade. They took these material things and concepts and employed them fruitfully for purposes of their own devising. That they were changed by these innovations is not to be gainsaid. What is to be emphasized here, however, is the point that the Indian was more or less in control of how these new ideas were to be incorporated into the ongoing culture. Because the power of the white man in their territory was still not a fact of prime importance, Indian peoples during fur-trading days (which varied as the white man moved across the continent) found much of value in the white man's tools and ideas.

In the eastern Woodlands we can find one example of how the fur trade provided Indians with both new technology and interesting ideas. Before the white man, decoration on clothing tended to be made with porcupine quills. Although they provided a beautiful and long-lasting form of decoration on items of apparel, working with such a difficult medium was time-consuming and limiting. Porcupine quills, for instance, are relatively stiff and cannot be worked in just any way. With the advent of colored beads from traders, though, the process of decorating items of clothing became much easier and new effects could be achieved with this more flexible medium. Life was made easier for the craftswoman and the result was exceptionally pleasing by any standard. Indeed, many connoisseurs of Indian art are keen enthusiasts of Indian beadwork—a form of art possible only after the arrival of the white man. In addition to this, many Indians became aware of new modes of decoration. While we are not sure of how Indian women became aware of the naturalistic art of the white man (perhaps Indian children studied representational art in early missionary schools or Indians espied the richly bro-caded robes of French priests), we do know that they began to borrow ideas from white models. In the Woodlands women began to bead designs of a more naturalistic flower type, generally known as floral beading. As a result of white influence, Indians began to see the flora and fauna of their environment in a more naturalistic vein and to realize this in beadwork form on their clothing. Thus, the tools and ideas of the white man in the early stages of contact had important effects on native arts and crafts.

Floral beading amongst the Woodlands Indians, narrative hide painting by men on the Great Plains, realistically beaded mounted warriors and national flags on items of clothing by women on the Great Plains, and a whole host of other developments exem-plify the effect of the white man's artistic notions on the peoples of North America. Pre-contact proclivities for abstraction, symbolism, and stylization came to coexist with new tendencies for the interpretation of objects as nearly as possible in their natural and everyday forms.

When the fur trade came to an end in a particular area, however, it usually meant the end of any balance between the Indian and his unfettered existence and the claims of white men for land to settle upon and exploit systematically. When this happened, as it inevitably did sooner or later, the Indian would be overwhelmed by the power and numbers of the white men. After either violent resistance or passive accept-ance, the Indian was settled on Indian reservations and forced to terminate many of his old modes of existence. This process of destroying the basis for Indian independence was especially difficult for the Plains Indian since he, quite clearly, had the most to lose from this new state of affairs. The despair and demoralization of Indian people confronted with the destruction of their older ways of life is hard to imagine. From our vantage point we can only attempt to comprehend the shattering sense of loss experi-enced by these people as they resigned themselves to meaningless lives of incarceration on reservations. There was no choice, really. They would either submit to the white man and accept a miserable existence on undesirable reserves or they would be exterminated right down to the last man, woman, and child.

The policy of restricting Indian peoples to isolated reservations became enforceable policy in both the United States and Canada by the 1870s. The implica-tions of reservation existence were clear: the Indian was to be shunted out of the way and made to be irrelevant to the national lives of the United States and Canada. The Ghost Dance Uprising of 1890 only demonstrated to Indian people, with the tragic events at Wounded Knee, South Dakota, that any sort of resistance to white authority would be crushed mercilessly. From the 1870s to the 1930s, Indian people felt powerless and neglected on a continent which they had once controlled and welcomed the white man to.

Concomitant with these events, many of the old arts and crafts fell into disuse or disfavor. Since Indian culture was widely ridiculed by a racist public opinion, and white missionaries and school teachers did their best to eradicate such qualities from their hapless charges, arts and crafts production deteriorated seriously both in terms of quantity and quality. While items everywhere were still produced for internal consumption, little encouragement was received from any quarter for the retention of traditional arts and crafts. The situation was aggravated by the availability of cheap white substitutes for almost everything the Indians once produced for themselves. If it were not for the dedicated efforts of Indian craftsmen them-selves to keep alive certain artistic traditions, and the efforts of far-seeing friends of the North American Indian, the traditions might have died away altogether. Nonetheless, they did not and today we can reap the harvest of those continuing traditions.

It was clear that the Indians would not just disappear or go away and cease to exist as a self-aware people. The 'Vanishing American' refused to vanish. Equally important, so too with many of his customs and traditions. Although his art has been vulgarized and cheapened by an undiscriminating tourist trade, quality survived the bleakest period of discourage-ment and oppression.

Today, especially as a result of the establishment of the Arts and Crafts Board of the Department of the Interior in 1935, Indian production is relatively high and quality in many instances is extraordinary. It must be emphasized, however, that arts and crafts produc-tion is a changed phenomenon from earlier times. Now Indian artisans produce for an art market and they are keenly sensitive to new situations and new structures.

In today's modern art world the Indian products which are in particularly high demand, both in North America and the world at large, are the following: Navajo rugs and silverwork; Pueblo jewelry and silver-work; Pueblo pottery from such villages as Acoma, San Ildefonso, Santa Clara, and Hano (from the Hopi group); contemporary Southwest and southern Plains painting, and Northwest Coast totemic carvings and masks. This is not to say that baskets, beadwork, ribbonwork, stonework, and the like are not being produced. On the contrary, they are—particularly for the growing groups of young white people who enjoy getting up in Indian garb for pow-wow celebrations. What is being emphasized here is that some articles are more commercially successful than others.

Insofar as the above is true, we have developing a phenomenon not unlike that which is characteristic for the art world as a whole. Indian artists of note, particularly those who possess inordinate skill or have

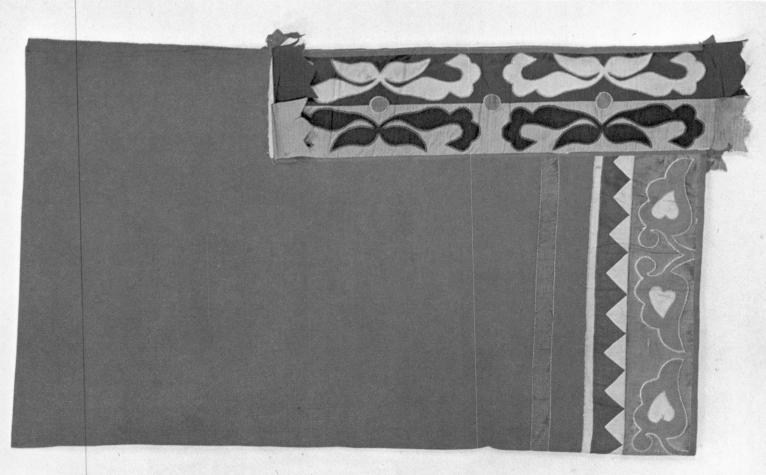

above 10. Buckskin pipe bag with beaded and quilled decoration. Length 28 in. Arapaho, Wyoming. Museum of the American Indian, Heye Foundation, New York

below 11. Red cloth robe with ribbonwork decoration. Length 31 in. Fox, Iowa. Museum of the American Indian, Heye Foundation, New York

a creative imagination far above the norm, have emerged to become 'names' in the specific fields of rugs, silverwork, pottery, woodcarving, or whatever. These individuals, who are artists in every sense of the word, are recognized for their excellence and their work tends to command very high prices. In fact, we have a situation where individual artisans are sought out more assiduously than the tribal designation under which they are categorized. Owning a Maria Martinez pot is more important than just a piece of pottery from San Ildefonso Pueblo. Owning a Bessie Many Goats tapestry, from the weaving center of Two Gray Hills, is more significant than obtaining just another Navajo rug. Owning a Ray Naha painting is more desirable than just having an example of Southwest Indian painting. And so it goes. When we come to search out the products of individual excellence rather than examples of traditional tribal production, we are truly in the realms of the modern art world.

What we are pointing to, though, is a tendency and not a universal fact as yet. There are still tribal traditions in arts and crafts that are very much alive. Not all artisans are 'names' or will become such. Yet, unattributed and anonymous art production goes against the grain of the modern art world and its commercial instincts. White buyers and connoisseurs like to know who has made a particular piece and the trend towards individual attribution of works is part and parcel of this matter. As the tendency grows, notable artists in the Indian community come to be represented more and more by exclusive outlets which have sole claim to their work. These galleries and studios will monopolize increasingly the truly excellent work being done by Indian artists.

What of mass production of Indian arts and crafts? This is a difficult question to address. In the near future there will be, most probably, a number of different tendencies. One trend will be for Indian people to gather together into cooperatives for the mass production of crafts of a specific sort. On the Canadian Plains, for example, a number of native-managed craft cooperatives have been established to engage in the mass production of moccasins, belts, gloves, necklaces, jackets, vests, and so on. The designing and decoration of these items will most likely become very standardized in order to appeal to mass tastes and conform to large marketing procedures. Another trend will be for individual entrepreneurs to hire Indian help to produce largely conventionalized Indian products which will nonetheless qualify for the 'Indian-made' label. It is very likely that a machine technology will be utilized quite heavily in this activity and any relationship between these products and traditional crafts will be coincidental. And finally, there will be a proliferation of outright machine-made 'fakes' and foreign imports purporting to be Indian-made goods. The latter is true not only of Hong-Kong-made 'beadwork' but of Mexican-made 'Navajo' rugs. In any case, it would appear as if there will be a growing difference between high quality items found only in galleries and studios

and mass-produced commodities which will be cheap but can only suggest what the traditional arts and crafts must have been like.

Of course, Indian arts and crafts of antique vintage will be made available when collections are offered for sale, but the prices which these goods will command will probably make them unavailable for anyone with average means. In sum, fine Indian art of an antique or contemporary nature, like any art, will rise in price as it becomes more avidly sought on the world's markets.

In terms of our survey of the life and art of the North American Indian, our approach will be one of a consideration of the various important cultural areas on the continent. While it is not always an ideal way of perceiving Indian life on the North American continent (that is, Indians north of Mexico), it nonetheless grants us some coherence in viewing a people who lived in proximity with each other and shared at least to some extent a common ecological basis and similar modes of livelihood. It can be said that the tribes who lived within a designated cultural area did share much in common and this quality of what is collectively true of their life is what is of importance to us.

The primary cultural areas to be dealt with in this volume are the following: the Southwest (in terms of both history and prehistory); the Southeast (mainly prehistory); the Plains; the Northwest Coast; the Woodlands; and finally, California and the Far West. This list is by no means exhaustive and excludes some areas of fair importance—for instance, the Great Basin and Plateau regions of North America. Nevertheless, our discussions will cover the major cultural areas of central importance in terms of artistic heritage. It is the collections we have from the above-named areas that form the bulk of museum inventories and have provided collectors and connoisseurs with the most gratification.

In investigating each cultural area we will attempt to examine something of the cultural life and history of the people in question and then discuss some of their outstanding contributions in arts and crafts. By now we do not need to emphasize the principle that the artistic culture of a people is a direct reflection of their mode of life in general, particularly the economic and ecological basis of that mode. How a tribe (and the people within it) provides for its fundamental needs of food, clothing, and shelter, and the ecological wherewithal which their environment offers, are key matters in the issue of human existence. Arts and crafts are fundamental reflections of that economic and ecological basis of tribal life.

In examining the various cultures of North America, we will want to be sensitive to the fact that not all Indians shared a common pattern of existence. As Olivia Vlahos has pointed out in her very useful introductory volume on Indians of the Americas, *New World Beginnings: Indian Cultures in the Americas*, there were at least four central modes of livelihood amongst Indian peoples north of Mexico. These varying ways of earning a living served as the basis for a cultural superstructure—such as religion, education, family and kinship structures, and so on. Since arts and crafts were a functional and utilitarian part of all Indian life, some are the actual economic tools for survival while other items are of less specifically economic import.

Vlahos identifies the following as the four major types of tribal occupations:

Hunters These are peoples who relied primarily on the flesh of various sorts of animals as the mainstay of their

siderable stability and durability. The Iroquois farmers of New York State or the Hopi farmers of Arizona can serve as examples of this mode of economic existence.

It goes without saying, of course, that some peoples combined two or more of these four types of possibilities in order to emerge with a hybrid mode of living. Nonetheless, the above serve as the four 'ideal types' of earning a living.

In carrying our discussion of the actual bases for arts and crafts further, we cannot ignore the fact that Indian culture bore an intrinsic relation to ecological

12. Piegan encampment. The Rocky Mountains can be seen in the background. Photograph by Edward S. Curtis

diet. From these animals they also obtained other necessities for existence such as skins for clothing and shelter. Sometimes the diet was supplemented by a certain amount of gathering of roots, berries, and other edible commodities. The Blackfeet who hunted buffalo upon the Plains or the Ojibway who hunted moose upon the Canadian Shield are examples of this type of people.

Fishermen These are peoples who lived primarily in coastal regions where rich stores of fish and other seafood could satisfy almost all dietary requirements. The Kwakiutl and Nootka fishermen of the Northwest Coast are prime examples of this kind of people.

Gatherers These are peoples who wandered nomadically about in search of edible flora and fauna in order to keep alive. Theirs was often a marginal existence fraught with hardship and difficulty. The Paiute of the Great Basin area are classic examples of these peoples.

Farmers More than is commonly thought, many Indian peoples were extremely successful farmers who provided for most of their needs by tilling the soil. In a variety of regions and under varying circumstances, several Indian tribes settled into sedentary (that is non-nomadic) existence in order to build societies of con-

realities. The Indian lived in particular environments and adapted to his surroundings with keen sensitivity. It has often been said that the North American Indian was the first and most natural ecologist we have known. In his mode of wresting a living from nature, the Indian was careful not to disrupt and destroy the natural basis of life within an area. His arts and crafts demonstrate that he possessed an uncanny ability to adapt to and use the natural resources of a particular region.

The major categories of artistic production point to the importance of natural materials and their availability in the Indian scheme of material culture. Andrew Hunter Whiteford wrote an excellent treatise on *North American Indian Arts* with the help of illustrator Owen Vernon Shaffer. In that small but very useful volume, Whiteford chose to classify Indian arts according to the natural materials used in the manufacture of particular items. Below is a brief summary of his schema:

Pottery From natural clays in various regions, Indians learned how to make containers of durability and beauty. Normally, pottery was made by peoples who lived in a relatively settled manner since pottery does not survive well under nomadic conditions. Pottery was produced primarily in the American Southwest, the Southeast, and Woodlands areas, and some was even manufactured in early times by farming tribes on the Plains. It was decorated in a bewildering variety of ways according to the artistic sense of the people in question. The North American Indian never devised the potter's wheel so all pottery was made by either the coiling or modeling and paddling methods.

Baskets North America abounded in natural fibers which lent themselves to various kinds of basketry. Strong archaeological evidence from the Southwest suggests that basketmaking predates pottery as a container form. Utilizing three basic techniques— plaiting, twining, and coiling—basketry is found in almost every cultural region in North America. The beauty of decoration on most baskets has made them avidly sought after by collectors everywhere.

Textiles This category includes a number of different items in which fibers of various sorts were woven into utilitarian objects. Both vegetable fibers and animal hairs were used in varying combinations depending on the region concerned. In the prehistoric Southwest, Pueblo farmers were growing cotton and weaving many of their basic items of clothing long before the coming of the white man. Navajo sheepherders have woven their famous rugs since the Spanish introduced sheep into the Southwest after 1600. Northwest Coast weavers of the Chilkat tribe wove gorgeous blankets of mountain sheep and dog hair. Sometimes the simple finger technique was employed and at others elaborate looms demanding considerable commitments of time and skill were used. The variety and type of North American weaving is quite extraordinary.

Skinwork While all Indians were hunters to some degree, it was mainly the tribes of the Plains and Woodlands who focused upon animals as a major source of food and clothing (and shelter, too, if we speak of the Plains). The hides of these animals provided the Indian with sufficient amounts of material for most of his clothing needs. On the Plains, the large hides of the buffalo also sufficed to provide those Indians with covering for their tipis. The skins could be prepared in such a way that they might be hard and thick (for parfleche carriers on the Plains) or soft and pliable for comfortable clothing. (Parfleche is rawhide soaked in lye to remove the hair.) The forms of decoration on such skins ranged from meager to lavish. Most of the time they were either painted or had porcupine quill or bead applied decoration. Sometimes all three forms of decoration were employed at once. The varieties of this form of craftwork are almost endless.

Woodwork Since forests covered much of North America, it is not surprising that wood crafts should occupy a position of some importance, particularly in the eastern Woodlands areas and the Pacific Northwest Coast. Tools, houses, ceremonial paraphernalia, eating utensils, sports equipment, and other items were made of this material. The bark of trees was utilized in eastern areas as containers. The decorative possibilities of wood, in terms of the carving that can be done, are almost infinite. Among the tribes of British Colombia and the panhandle of Alaska carving reached heights of artistic attainment that have rarely been equalled by any people.

Bonework As important by-products of animals killed for their meat and hides, bones provided many supplementary tools for the Indian. A listing of bone tools would include mention of projectile points, needles and pins, weaving tools, scrapers, chisels, tubular instruments, ornaments, fishhooks, items for games of chance, utensils, hair pipes, and the like. Although the artistic merit of many of these objects might be slight, they were nonetheless important for economic and functional needs.

Stonework Here was a material of vast importance for a people whose technological development never reached much into the metal age. As tools, stone provided the bulk of material worked by these people. By chipping, pecking, grinding, and cutting operations, they fashioned such things as projectile points, spear points, knife blades, celts (hand axes), scrapers, hoes, pipes, effigies, and so on. A number of objects whose use is problematical but which are termed 'birdstones' and 'bannerstones' because of their shape were also made.

Shellwork From the coastal areas of North America came a bewildering variety of shells which were used as ornamentation in a myriad of ways. The prehistoric peoples were particularly resourceful in the decoration of shells: the Southeastern mound dwellers engraved large conch shells with designs reminiscent of the central Valley of Mexico, and the Hokoham peoples in the Southwest incised clam shells to achieve beautiful effects. Smaller shells, like those of the oliva and cowrie sort, were used for necklaces or incorporated into embroidered designs on clothing.

Metalwork Although the Indian peoples never achieved a real metal culture, at the time of European discovery several Indian cultures knew how to use copper for decorative purposes. As early as 5000 BC, tribes in the Great Lakes region made interesting copper tools (like celts) using primitive techniques. Mound dwellers made distinctive ceremonial plaques using thin sheets of copper. In the 1870s the Spanish introduced silver into the Southwest and Navajo craftsmen began using it to make lovely pieces of jewelry, a tradition now very much developed amongst the Navajo and some of their Pueblo neighbors.

Featherwork Many tribes throughout North America utilized the beautiful plumage of birds in order to decorate themselves, for both personal and ceremonial reasons. Personal adornment amongst Plains Indians was particularly well-developed and everyone is familiar with the famous Sioux warbonnets of the classic period. In the Southwest, the Pueblo people used bird feathers to decorate the sacred costumes of the Katchina deities, and in California the Hupa and Yarok peoples made impressive headgear from the feathers of local birds. The Pomo tribe of California covered their tightly woven baskets with tiny feathers plucked **14** from local songbirds.

While this list of ten types of craft forms is not exhaustive, it does serve to suggest how the Indian always utilized the natural materials of his environment in order to carry on the task of existence and introduce some beauty in that process as well.

With this brief discussion of some general points of significance relating to Indian arts, we are now ready to begin a more detailed survey of the life and art of the North American Indian. We will begin by looking at the prehistoric cultures.

The prehistoric civilizations

The term 'prehistoric' has strong ethnocentric overtones as it relates to the study of Indian cultures in North America. It is a name applied to all Indian life as it existed before the 'discovery' of the Americas by the Europeans in 1492 (Leif Ericson notwithstanding, it would seem). Thus, the designation 'prehistoric' is usually intended to refer to those Indian cultures which existed from earliest times in North America to around AD 1500. Since the Indians north of Mexico had no written records of any sort (depending as they did on their oral traditions) there is no documentation about their life before the advent of European explorers and adventurers. Insofar as this is true, our knowledge about these peoples relies almost wholly upon the efforts of archaeologists to reconstruct clues about their existence based on material remains. It is from the spadework of archaeologists, then, that we obtain information of fundamental import about the life of peoples who existed before the accounts of early European visitors.

Very little is known about the origins of man in the New World. Most scholars are fairly well agreed that man was not indigenous to the Americas but came to these shores from the Old World. The exact dates of his coming, however, are locked in the vaults of prehistory. It is thought by most that the earliest settlers must have slowly found their way across the Bering Strait from Siberia to Alaska sometime between 10,000 and 65,000 years ago. During the Pleistocene Epoch in geologic history (an epoch which began some 1,500,000 years ago), four successive ice sheets advanced and retreated across the face of the North American continent. In the last of these great glacial periods, the Wisconsin ice sheet, man found his way from the Asian heartland into the American hinterland.

Insofar as ice periods perforce utilize great quantities of water for the development of their glaciers, it is believed that the Wisconsin period must have tied up a sufficient amount of the earth's water supply to lower the level of the northern seas by several hundreds of feet. It is estimated that the level of the Bering Sea could have been anywhere from 150 to 300 feet lower than what it is today. If this were so, what is now called the Bering Strait, a narrow body of water lying between the Chukchi Peninsula of Siberia and the Seward Peninsula of Alaska, would have been, in actuality, a strip of land some 300 to 1000 miles wide. In other words, Asia and America at one time were contiguous land masses, and early peoples could not possible have been aware of the fact that they were 'emigrating' from one continent to another.

It was only 10,000 years ago (not very long in geologic history) that the climate of the earth warmed up to a point where the ice receded to its present locations and the Bering Strait came to lie permanently under water. Prior to that time, we believe, nomadic bands of hunting and gathering peoples found their way through natural migration patterns to the mainland of what we now know as North America. There was no one great exodus of masses of people from Asia but a continuous, if haphazard, penetration to search out the Ice-Age mammals such as the sabertooth tiger, long-tusked mammoth, mastodon, cameloids, giant sloths, and to gather the bounty of an unexploited natural environment.

Indeed, climatological research suggests that areas of Alaska and Canada could have been warmer during certain periods of the last Ice Age than they are today. The result of this must have been that there were many excellent valleys and ice-free corridors (perhaps paralleling the Yukon River and continuing down on the eastern side of the Rocky Mountains) that allowed these people to pass. In such a way, no doubt, did the native peoples of North America find their way from the Bering Strait to Tierra del Fuego at the tip of South America. When the last big glacial melt began in 8000 BC, the water level of the Bering Sea gradually rose and the two continents were separated. By that time, however, it is probable that the ancestors of the North American Indian were already dispersed throughout the new continent.

Be that as it may, we know that prehistoric man was on the continent of North America before the end of the Wisconsin glacial period. While we could focus on several developments at this time all over the existent land mass, we shall concentrate our attention on two areas where civilizations capable of outstanding artistic output existed: the American Southwest and the American Southeast.

The Southwest

The three most notable cultures that grew up and flourished in this region were the Mogollon, the Hohokam, and the Anasazi. How they developed and the kind of arts which they produced will occupy our attention in this important section.

The dating of archaeological sites has always been a difficult process. Since we are not dealing with cultures which could leave us a written record of their existence, we have had to utilize less direct means of obtaining dates for them. Two methods most frequently employed in the Southwest have been dendrochronology and radiocarbon dating.

16. Shell gorget with design showing a warrior apparently
dancing with the head of his victim. 1200–1600. Diameter 4 in.
Castalian Springs, Sumner County, Tennessee. Museum
of the American Indian, Heye Foundation, New York

17

18

19

20

21

Arizona astronomer A. E. Douglass, interested in the effects of sunspots on vegetation growth in the Southwest, inadvertently provided archaeology with one of its most reliable forms of dating prehistoric villages. Utilizing trees as his major subject-matter, Douglass noticed that it was not difficult to tell the age of trees by recourse to their growth rings. In each year of its life a tree grows, and as it does so it adds a ring of that growth to its diameter. In years of a lot of rain, the tree ring is significantly wide; in years of little rain, the tree ring is clearly much thinner. Douglass found this fact interesting in terms of his research on the effect of sunspots. For archaeologists, it had further significance. Since one could tell the age of a tree when it was felled merely by counting its tree rings, a basic clue could be had as to the age of Pueblo villages which used trees as roof beams as a part of their construction. When a continuous sequence of reliable tree ring dates was worked out on a master chart, archaeologists could ascertain the age of a village they were exploring if they could obtain a decent log from that village. A master chart exists which can trace tree ring growths in the Southwest back to 59 BC.

A second mode of dating is found in the radiocarbon technique. Based on the work of Willard F. Libby, the central idea is that all living organisms contain a radioactive isotope of carbon which is called carbon 14. When they are alive all organisms contain about the same amount of carbon 14, and when they die carbon 14 is released at a constant rate from these organisms as they decompose. Utilizing atomic-age science and technology, the decomposition rate of carbon 14 has been calculated to the degree that one can now tell how long an organism has been dead. Thus archaeologists can take a bit of charcoal from ancient fires and determine the approximate time when those fires were lit in Indian fireplaces. It is a fascinating process.

With these scientific tools at hand, archaeologists have been hard at work to unlock the secrets of ancient life in the Southwest. While they have not always possessed such sophisticated methods, pioneers have been in the field since before the turn of the century.

One of the most interesting theories to emerge of late as the result of intensive scientific work in the Casas Grandes region of the Southwest (located in the northern part of the Mexican state of Sonora, adjacent to Arizona) has been put forward by Charles C. Di Peso of the Amerind Foundation. It is his central contention that the entire area of Mexico north of the central Valley of Mexico to the upper limits of the Southwest cultural region in Utah and Colorado should be known as the Gran Chichimeca. The Southwest, as we know, conventionally covers the states of Arizona and New Mexico along with the very southern portions of Utah and Colorado. His argument centers on the notion that, in point of fact, this area is the northern part of a whole cultural unit in Meso-American history.

Even more importantly, Di Peso feels that there was a particular set of relationships within this cultural whole. To be specific, he says, evidence suggests that the Valley of Mexico was a kind of metropolis to the hinterland areas of the American Southwest. As a metropolis, the Valley of Mexico was the true source of culture, commerce, technology, government, and stylistic innovations for the hinterland of the north.

From the Valley of Mexico radiated the ideas and goods which were to influence developments in the periphery sector of the north. Of course, in order to sustain itself as a metropolis and safeguard its central power, the Valley of Mexico had to exploit economically the hinterland potentials in the American Southwest. This meant that power in certain real ways, particularly commercial power, had to be exercised.

In his short pamphlet published by the Museum of New Mexico Press entitled *Casas Grandes and the Gran Chichimeca*, Di Peso develops his thesis with persuasiveness. To simplify his exposition rather brutally, Di Peso points out that the Southwest had some importance as an exploitable area to the trading base in the Valley of Mexico. The Southwest could have been an important supplier of turquoise gem stones, slaves, peyote, salt, salenite, and other frontier products. In return, the people of the hinterland received numerous cultural influences from the metropolis such as warrior cremations, pyrite mirrors, clay figurines, formalized city plans, massive irrigation projects, ceremonial mounds, and ball courts (where two matched teams could play ball games not wholly unlike modern hockey or lacrosse). That the exchange was an unequal one between metropolis and hinterland is a foregone conclusion. All this can be seen with particular effect, he argues, in the case of the Hohokam peoples.

While there was indigenous development in the American Southwest before Valley of Mexico influence became dominant, Di Peso suggests that this area could have come within the Mexican sphere of influence by AD 750. Around 900 to 1050, the Tezcatlipoca-influenced Toltec families might have possessed extensive power in the Casas Grandes, Gila-Salt River, and Chaco Canyon areas of Arizona and New Mexico. From 1050 to around 1340, the Quetzalcoatl influence of the Toltec peoples could have extended even further among the Hohokam/Mogollon/Anasazi peoples. Taking over from the Toltecs, the Aztecs (around 1340) probably consolidated a new rule, termed Huitzilopochtli by Di Peso, over the entire area.

Although the Spanish conquistadores liquidated Aztec power with Cortez's victory over Montezuma in 1520, the American Southwest simply shifted over to their sovereignty when it was expressed with Coronado's expedition in 1540. Until the United States federal government took over the area from Mexico in the 1840s, the area remained under the sway of the Valley of Mexico with a grip unbroken since AD 750. Then Washington DC became the new metropolis for these hapless people.

It is a fascinating and provocative thesis. While whole sections of it remain to be proved, it provides us with the first complete framework for interpreting and understanding relationships in the prehistoric world. With a scope and explanatory power hitherto unattempted, Di Peso has sought to meaningfully interrelate cultures within an entire region of the New World. His interpretation of those relationships as a mercantilistic system provides us with real cause-and-effect explanations of a complex reality.

Considering strictly the development of the Southwest, however, we are presented with a complex problem of understanding how early man planted the seeds of civilization which were to ripen into the cultures of the Hohokam, Mogollon, and Anasazi.

17. Large red ware bowl with a strong swirling pattern in the interior. 900–1000. Diameter 11 in. Mogollon, Gila County, Arizona. Museum of the American Indian, Heye Foundation, New York

18. Pottery jar with red painted decoration. 900–1100. Height 5 in. Hohokam, Pinal County, Arizona. Museum of the American Indian, Heye Foundation, New York

19. Black-on-white ware bowl, the decoration showing a man and woman under a blanket. Diameter 10.25 in. Mimbres, New Mexico. Museum of the American Indian, Heye Foundation, New York

20. Zoomorphic effigy vessel. 1100–1300. Height 9 in. Anasazi, Tularosa Canyon, New Mexico. Museum of the American Indian, Heye Foundation, New York

21. Pottery pitcher with black-on-white decoration. Height 7.5 in. Peñasca Blanca Pueblo, Chaco Canyon, New Mexico. Museum of the American Indian, Heye Foundation, New York

Tentative thinking by several leading archaeologists informs us that these three cultures had earlier predecessors. From the evidence of various finds, we believe man could have arrived in the Southwest around 35,000 BC. In terms of more substantial evidence, it seems as if there were two distinct traditions in the Southwest before the time of Christ. Archaeologists call the older of the two, which could date back to 14,000 BC, the Paleo-Indian Tradition and the younger of the two, which could date back to 9000 BC, the Desert Tradition. From 9000 BC to around 4000 BC, they could have existed side by side in the region of the Southwest.

The Paleo-Indian Tradition is one of hunters. In that kind of time period we know that the Southwest was considerably less arid than it is today. They were probably big game hunters who sought such now extinct animals as the mammoth. Several specific types of this man have been identified including Sandia Man (12,000 BC), Clovis Man (11,000 BC), Folsom Man (7500 BC), and Portales Man (4500 BC). Each of these differing stages of the Paleo-Indian Tradition saw the man of that epoch producing distinctive stone projectile points which are an identifying hallmark. We are not sure what happened to these men or what became of their tradition.

The Desert Tradition is much more important to us insofar as understanding the origins of prehistoric civilization is concerned. The Desert people lived to the west of the Paleo-Indians and had a primarily foraging economy, although they probably also did some kind of hunting. From the evidence they left behind in caves across the area, we discern that their material culture was rich in baskets, sandals, mats, netting, and so on. Enough of their culture is known to divide it into three developments: the Sulphur Springs Cochise, the Chiricahua Cochise, and the San Pedro Cochise. (The reader should not confuse the labelling of these prehistoric cultures with the Apache chief of the same name who lived in the 19th century. They are quite different entities, although romantic-minded scholars must have been moved by the fame of the late Apache warrior to so name these very early cultures.)

What is important about the Desert Tradition, we believe, is that it gave birth to the earliest culture of the Southwest: the Mogollon. We are also of the opinion that it gave rise to the Hohokam tradition as well. Thus, the Desert Tradition appears to have been a seminal force in the prehistoric Southwest.

The Mogollon people

Shortly before the time of Christ in the Southwest, certain of the Desert tribes began to acquire from Mexico the seeds and technology for the cultivation of crops. As most of the world knows, New World agriculturists made a significant contribution to modern diets with a number of innovations unknown to the Old World. Without the genius and efforts of the Indian of the Americas, the world would be without the following important crops: corn, squash, potatoes, beans (of certain varieties), tomatoes, strawberries, chocolate, avocados, and many, many more. The

particular staple crops of the prehistoric Southwest were corn, beans, and squash. After a while, they also began the cultivation of cotton which was a continuous crop with the Pueblo people right up until 1900 when they began to turn to commercial varieties. In any case, up from Mexico to Arizona and New Mexico came the technology for the beginnings of agriculture.

Around 300 BC, in the region of the Mogollon Mountains of western New Mexico and eastern Arizona, a group of the San Pedro Cochise people began to build pit houses, practise agriculture, manufacture pottery, and live in a more or less sedentary vein. Thus was born the Mogollon tradition.

Their pit houses were relatively simple affairs, being from two to five feet deep and quadrangular in shape. Sometimes a larger village would have as many as 26 of these houses within it. They were among the first of the Southwest peoples to devise the principle of the religious underground ceremonial chamber which has come to be called a *kiva*. The word derives from the Hopi language and refers generally to any large room primarily used for religious purposes. For the most part these *kivas* were circular in shape and located almost wholly underground. Entrance was by means of a ladder through the roof. Inside such a chamber, men (and men only) would meet to perform secret ceremonial rituals, teach young boys the ways of the Pueblo, and engage in other religious activities. In addition to these more serious endeavors, the *kiva* was a kind of men's club room where they could meet to talk, enjoy each other's fellowship, and produce various arts and crafts. The *kiva* was the very heart of Puebloan religious and ceremonial life. The *kiva* perhaps served as a reminder to the people of their origins below the surface of the earth. (The modern Hopi people have a myth that many worlds exist, in layers, below the surface of the earth and that their ancestors lived in these worlds before they reached the present level.)

Although the Mogollon people lived in their hilly domain for some 1300 years, their culture changed but little during this entire period. Their general conservatism, in fact, is one of their primary characteristics. Although archaeologists have denoted them as traversing through five cultural stages, the change from one stage to another was not dramatic.

Around the last cultural stage, however, it is clear that the Mogollon were virtually absorbed by the more vigorous and outgoing Anasazi to the north. The Mogollon abandoned their exclusive pit house style and began building masonry Pueblos like the Anasazi. By about 1100, the Mogollon were an integral part of the Great Pueblo phase of the dominant Anasazi peoples.

The most important contribution the Mogollon made to the arts is their pottery (as might also be said of the Hohokam and Anasazi, although with less assurance due to other notable achievements). Before the Mogollon 5 period, they produced a predominantly plain or **17** polished red ware which, while pleasant enough, is not very intriguing. Available evidence indicates that these people—and perhaps the San Pedro Cochise Desert people who preceded them—learned the art of pottery-

making from Mexican Indians. While their pottery styles changed somewhat over time, it was not until phase 5 that they began to make a truly distinguished pottery product.

During Mogollon 5 the Mimbres branch of these people, heavily influenced by Anasazi black-on-white styles of ceramics, began to make a type of pottery that has captured the affection of connoisseurs everywhere. They manufactured bowls in great numbers and decorated their interiors with finely drawn designs illustrating birds, animals, people, and scenes. While **19, 27, 28** these designs are executed in a highly stylized manner, they obviously possess a great amount of charm, technical perfection, beauty, and even humor. Not all of the bowls were decorated with anthropomorphic or zoomorphic designs. Several of them contained abstract and symbolic motifs executed with exquisite finesse. Many experts consider this particular style of pottery from the Mimbres phase of the Mogollon culture to be the finest expression of ceramic art in prehistoric America. While it is not necessary to debate the matter, we can agree that this pottery is worthy of the highest praise. Why it came about and why it suddenly disappeared, we do not know. It is a mystery.

The Hohokam people

The Hohokam were, like their neighbors the Mogollon, influenced by the Desert Tradition. They appeared on the scene around the time of Christ and existed as a viable culture until about AD 1400. During their 1400 years of existence, the Hohokam passed through four distinct stages of cultural evolution: (1) the Pioneer (AD 1–600); (2) the Colonial (600–900); (3) the Sedentary (900–1100); and (4) the Classic (1100–1400).

Like the Mogollon, the Hohokam peoples built large pit houses, although theirs were bigger and more shallow. Although they lived in an extremely arid portion of southern Arizona (around the present-day location of Phoenix), they carried on a successful program of agriculture. As early as the Colonial period they were building irrigation ditches which could carry the water of the Gila River to their parched crops. By the Sedentary period this irrigation complex had reached impressive proportions, both in terms of engineering skill and in the area covered by this network of canals. Considering the fact that these people had little more than stone tools and their backs with which to build these projects, their attainments become all the more noteworthy.

As for their material culture, the Hohokam were skilled workers in the shell arts, stone, and pottery. In **18** the early Pioneer phase of their culture they produced little clay figurines which show a strong Mexican influence. In fact, as Di Peso has already pointed out for us, the issue of Mexican cultural presence is a real one for the Hohokam since we are confronted at every turn with evidence of their influence. Their use of stone palettes for the mixing of color pigments, the existence of ball courts, mirrors, and so on demonstrate a strong relationship of some sort to Mexican Indians.

When we turn to their ceramics, we are presented

opposite 25. Polychrome bowl with fret design. Height 4·75 in.
St Johns, Arizona. Museum of the American Indian,
Heye Foundation, New York

below 26. Red-on-buff ware vessel with geometric decoration.
Height 11 in. Hohokam, Pinal County, Arizona. Museum of
the American Indian, Heye Foundation, New York

with a tradition of extremely fine red-on-buff pottery. **26**
As we can tell from the illustration in this book, their
sense of proportion and design is unique in North
America. It was during the Sedentary period that red-
on-buff pottery achieved its greatest development
with decorations consisting of interlocking patterns of
human and geometric forms. Occasionally, during
this period, huge jars were made which could hold up
to thirty gallons, although sometimes these very large
ollas were used to hold the ashes of the dead. (The
Hohokam cremated their deceased members and put
their ashes into pottery receptacles.) Clay figurines also
continued to be made during this period, with a greater
emphasis on naturalism.

The arts were well-developed in the Hohokam culture by the Sedentary period. In shellwork, for example,
bracelets were made and they had learned to etch
designs on clam shells by applying an acid solution
made from cactus (a technique perfected some 300
years before Europeans learned it). Pottery, stone
vessels and palettes, copper bells, and other items are
found in significant numbers and all portray some sign
of Mexican influence.

By the fourth stage (the Classic phase), the Hohokam
came under the influence of the Anasazi peoples, just
like the Mogollon before them. During the Classic
period there were two waves of Anasazi peoples from
the north who came to dwell amongst the Hohokam.
From the Flagstaff area came Sinagua peoples and
from Tonto Basin came Salado peoples. These dual
invasions of Anasazis appear to have been peaceful
since there is no evidence of bloodshed or warfare.
Also, the Anasazi people built their multistoried
dwellings amidst the older Hohokam pit houses, with
little evidence of any sort of disruption. It was the

Salado people who built Casa Grande which is now a famous ruin located just south of Phoenix, Arizona.

By about 1400, the Hohokam begin to disappear from history. Where did they go and what happened to them? We are not sure of the answer. Some archaeologists believe they might have gone south into the northern portions of the present-day Mexican state of Sonora where, with the remaining elements of the Mogollon, they collectively established the short-lived Casas Grandes culture. Others believe they simply deteriorated as a viable culture giving rise to the contemporary Pima and Papago Indians who live on the desert much as the Hohokam must have done in their Pioneer period. Whatever happened to these fascinating people, by 1500 we have little trace of them remaining in the Southwest.

The Anasazi people

Among the prehistoric peoples of the Southwest, none are more famed, honored, or researched than the Anasazi. The name was given to them by Navajo herdsmen who now occupy their once vast domain, and it means 'The Ancient Ones.' The heartland area of Anasazi habitation was basically around the Four Corners area where New Mexico, Colorado, Arizona, and Utah meet at a common point. There, in the drainage of the San Juan River and its tributaries, lived a people who have achieved note because of their superlative architecture and outstanding ceramic arts. The relics of their culture—the great ghost-like ruins of ancient Pueblos and cliff villages which they built – are visited annually by thousands of people.

Little is known about the actual origins of the Anasazi. In their long tenure of existence in the Southwest, however, we are fairly sure that these people were the direct ancestors of the contemporary Puebloan Indians. Thus there is a direct and continuous tradition between the Anasazi people and the Indians who currently live in Pueblos in the New Mexico and Arizona region of the United States.

We know, further, that the Anasazi people who built the great Pueblos and cliff cities of the Four Corners area did not come into existence with a fully developed culture. Their splendid capabilities in architecture and the ceramic arts were the result of a very long period of evolution—perhaps influenced by the Mogollon, Hohokam, and Mexican cultures. The gestation period required before the great Pueblos were built is estimated to be around 900 years at least. In order to better comprehend the evolutionary development of the Anasazi people, archaeologists have divided their history into Basketmaker and Pueblo periods.

Some archaeologists, like Irving Rouse, speculate that the Anasazi culture may have come out of the Desert Tradition as did the Mogollon and Hohokam. If this is so, however, the evidence is quite scanty and the hypothesis must be a tentative one. Be that as it may, the Anasazi came to be a powerful and influential people who literally overwhelmed the other neighboring cultures of the American Southwest. Their dominance becomes manifest around 1100 and continues on from that point.

Because we are aware of the distinct Basketmaker and Pueblo variations in the history of the Anasazi, a number of different classifications have been put forward in order to divide up their history and make their development more coherent. Two of the most important of these are the Pecos Classification of 1927 and the Frank H. H. Roberts, Jr, typology of 1935. Since readers of this book will likely encounter both classifications in various studies and museum exhibitions, we will briefly list both below. Both are heuristic but we will utilize the Roberts' modification of the Pecos Classification for the purposes of our commentary.

It is very difficult to give absolute time periods for any of these stages of Anasazi development since evolution varied from region to region. In the Chaco Canyon area of New Mexico, for example, develop-

ment from Basketmaker to the Great Pueblo period was very quick and the peak of this culture occurred much earlier here than elsewhere. By the year 1000 the Great Pueblo communities of Chaco Canyon (like Pueblo Bonito) were already in existence while in regions like Mesa Verde or the Navajo National Monument such communities were to emerge later. Thus, dating procedures have to be subject to local variations.

In any case, let us briefly summarize each stage of Anasazi development and correlate this to the arts typical of each period.

Pecos Classification	Roberts' Modification
Basketmaker I	
Basketmaker II	Basketmaker
Basketmaker III	Modified Basketmaker
Pueblo I	
Pueblo II	Developmental Pueblo
Pueblo III	Great Pueblo
Pueblo IV	Regressive Pueblo
Pueblo V	Historic Pueblo

Basketmaker Around the time of Christ a people begin to emerge in the area of the San Juan drainage whom archaeologists have chosen to call the Basketmaker. These people have been so named because they produced finely woven baskets of truly exceptional quality and beauty. The arid climate of the Southwest has caused many of these baskets to survive until the present. Although potterymaking was apparently unknown to these people, most of their container needs were very likely fulfilled by the variety of baskets which they were able to weave. They possessed an agricultural technology which is exemplified in the remains of simple forms of corn from this period. Their mode of living was quite simple, being confined to brush shelters or the protection of caves. They stored their crops in pits lined with stone slabs for future consumption, and possibly supplemented what they grew with the gathering of various sorts of roots and nuts. The

general period of their occupancy dates from AD 1 to around 400.

Modified Basketmaker What sets these people apart from the preceding stage is a number of significant developments in cultural complexity. For one thing, they now became more settled and lived in abodes of more substance, that is true pit-dwellings with slab lining for durability. New and better forms of corn were introduced during this time and beans became a regular produce.

It is also during this period that we witness the beginnings of true pottery amongst the Anasazi. Whereas we are quite sure that the Mogollon and Hohokam developed their ceramics from Mexican sources, there is some question as to how pottery became a part of the material culture of the Anasazi. There does not seem to be any evidence for the hypothesis that pottery was introduced into this culture from elsewhere. On the contrary, it is entirely possible that these people went through the complete process of inventing ceramic wares for themselves. Collections of Modified Basketmaker material show an interesting sequence of possible developments that might have led to the emergence of true pottery.

There are examples of Modified Basketmaker baskets which show that the women must have lined many of them with clay in order to make them more watertight. From certain remains, we can surmise that some of these baskets must inevitably have come too near the fire to prevent combustion. When this happened, it is apparent that the basket fibers would burn away but the clay in the interior of the bowl would be made far more hard as a result of the fire's heat. These people must have learned from such accidents that heat applied to clay would produce a very hard and durable form of container. We have examples in various collections where the imprinted marks of the basket still remain on the surface of hardened pottery. It is entirely possible that Modified Basketmaker women first produced pottery—after the initial discovery—by actually

*31. Polychrome bowl with painted parrot design. Diameter
11 in. Hawikuh, New Mexico. Museum of the American
Indian, Heye Foundation, New York*

going through the process of weaving a basket, lining it with clay, and then burning away the basket exterior in a baking or firing operation. It seems that after a while they found out that it was unnecessary to go through the laborious process of making a basket first since they could begin immediately with the act of shaping a bowl. This very probably was the way in which potterymaking came to the earliest Anasazi people.

After the craft of ceramics was learned, these people soon began to provide simple decorations for their wares. For the most part, the background was a dull kind of gray with painted designs in black appearing on it. The most common types of pottery we have from this period, identified by the general style of decoration, are the following: Lino Black-on-Gray, Lino Gray, Abajo Red-on-Orange (possibly influenced by the Mogollon), and plain, unslipped bowls. In artistic terms, the pottery is not very important.

The time span for the Modified Basketmaker period is approximately 400–700. From the historical development of this Basketmaker culture, the stage was now set for the emergence of a true Pueblo life style.

Developmental Pueblo These Indians began to build houses that went beyond the slab-lined pit houses of their immediate ancestors. Major innovations in masonry and architecture were introduced with the tendency towards single-room dwellings in multiroom Pueblos. Some structures were still made of slabs while others employed a more developed technology of adobe bricks or wattle-and-daub construction.

In the field of pottery, significant advances were recorded both in technology and decoration. In the Developmental period we find the classic white-slipped background appearing with a strong-lined black paint applied over it. Here is where we locate what is to become the hallmark of Anasazi decorated ware: the Black-on-White design schema. Examples of this sort are the following: Reserve Black-on-White, White Mound Black-on-White, Mancos Black-on-White, Black Mesa Black-on-White, and so on. During this period, a utilitarian type of 'corrugated' ware was made for cooking and storage in which the spiral coils on the outside of the bowl provide the only decoration.

Kivas also start appearing in the prototype Pueblo villages coming into existence during this period. Their location underground can be accounted for by two possible explanations. Firstly, the Pueblo Indians held to a creation myth which explained their origins upon the earth as the result of successive existences in four layers beneath the present surface of the earth. In each *kiva* there would be a small hole—designated as the *sipapu*—to symbolize their emergence from the previous dwelling place in the underworld. A second explanation is found in the fact that the Pueblo people first built their habitations underground and therefore might have felt that such an architectural feature was tied up with their historic and mythological past. In either case, the occurrence of *kivas* becomes a trademark of all Pueblo villages in succeeding generations of these people. Each clan in a village had its own *kiva* with distinctive ceremonial functions and duties attendant to each single chamber.

Although basketry declined as a craft form during this era, the cultivation of cotton developed, and hence cotton fabrics began to make their appearance in the Anasazi world.

The approximate time period for the Developmental Pueblo epoch is 700–1100.

Great Pueblo This is the period when some of the developments mentioned before come to full maturity. In architecture, for example, masonry was sophisticated enough to allow for the construction of multistoried apartment-like dwellings. Great circular *kivas* of unparalleled size and impressiveness also appeared during the Great Pueblo time.

During this distinguished period of Southwestern prehistory, many of the great sites which are now visited by tourists came to be built. In the Chaco Canyon area we can find such Puebloan cities as Pueblo Bonito; in Mesa Verde there are Cliff Palace, Spruce Tree House, Balcony House, Cedar Tree Tower, Far View Ruins, and Sun Point Pueblo; in the Kayenta region there are Betatakin, Keet Seel, and Inscription House Ruin; not to mention such individually important ruins as Tuzigoot, Montezuma's Castle, Aztec Ruins, Tonto, Walnut Canyon, Wupatki, and many others too numerous to mention.

23, 24

Some of the Great Pueblo communities, like Pueblo Bonito, are largely communities built on the fertile floors of wide canyons and valleys. Other communities, like Cliff Palace or Montezuma's Castle, are built high up in the natural caves located on the sides of precipitous cliffs. Since the Chaco Canyon complex was a bit earlier than most of the others, we gain the impression that the Pueblo peoples faced problems of security sometime after 1100. More and more, we find, they began to select secluded locations for their villages, with an eye towards easy defensibility. It is entirely possible that the northern Athapaskan ancestors of present-day Navajo and Apache Indians began to infiltrate the Southwest area during the period 1100 to 1300. If so, they must have raided the Pueblo peoples extensively and generally made life miserable for them. Tempting booty like women captives, plentiful crops, superb arts and crafts and so on must have lured these Athapaskans mightily.

During this same time we find, at last, tangible evidence that the Anasazi were in contact with Meso-American influences and were receiving all kinds of trade goods from Mexican sources. In fact, trade relations with many different regions seem to be pretty well established by this time. Shells of all sorts were brought into the Anasazi realm from the Gulf of Mexico and the California coast. With these items Pueblo artisans fashioned exquisite jewelry and sometimes utilized these shells as the basis for intricate turquoise stone inlay work. There is persuasive evidence to the effect that trade relations with the prehistoric Southeastern peoples were in force as early as the Developmental Pueblo period. From these sources the Anasazi could have received the ideas for effigy jars, hollow ring bowls, and other items of Southeastern derivation. It was during the Great Pueblo epoch that we find Anasazi culture extending its influence and domain over a very wide region of the Southwest, ultimately absorbing the Mogollon and Hohokam peoples.

40

20

Also in this period we find pottery carried to new heights of excellence and variety. A thin, hard, and often polished form of pottery was produced all over the Anasazi realm in the Great Pueblo time. There was a great deal of regional specialization, so much so that

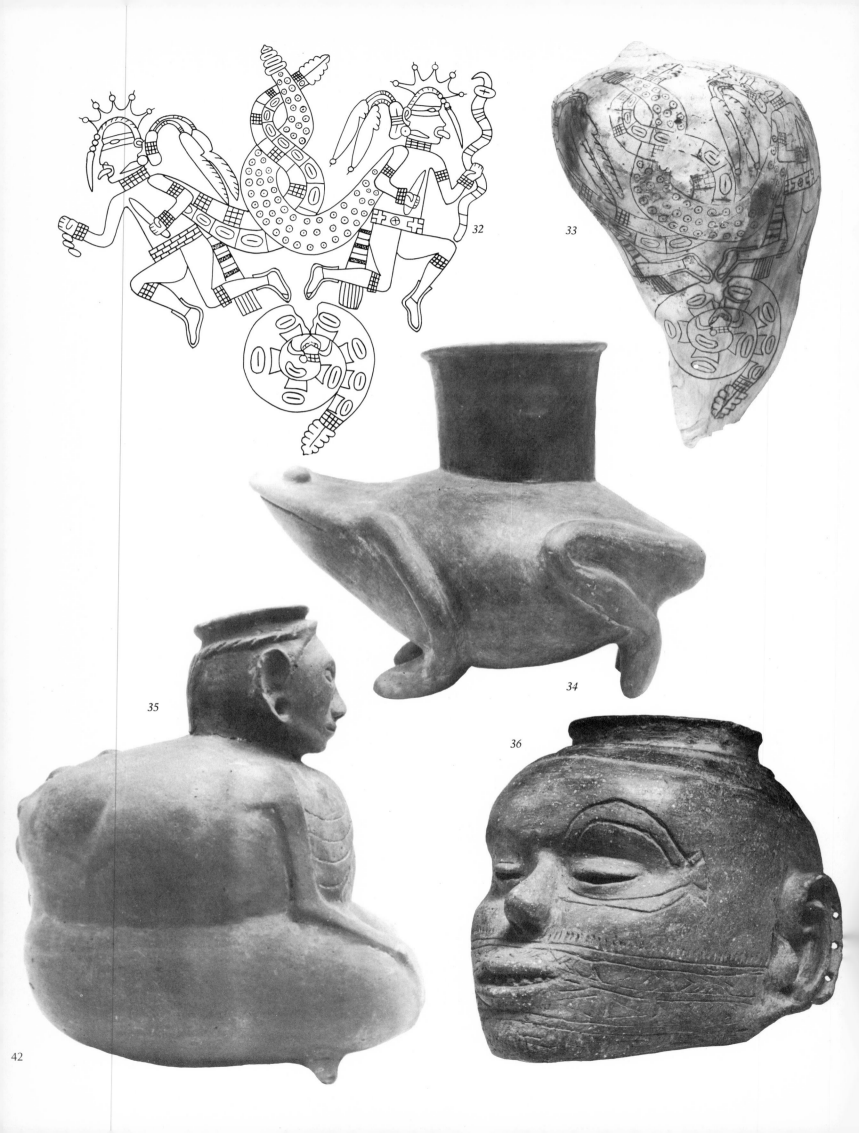

32

33

34

35

36

42

32. Design on conch shell, see 33.

33. Conch shell with incised decoration. 1200–1600. Length 12·5 in. Spiro Mound, Le Flore County, Oklahoma. Museum of the American Indian, Heye Foundation, New York

34. Jar in the form of a frog. 1200–1600. Height 7·5 in. Mississippi County, Arkansas. Museum of the American Indian, Heye Foundation, New York

35. Jar in the form of a hunchback figure. Height 8·5 in. Crittenden County, Arkansas. Museum of the American Indian, Heye Foundation, New York

36. Death's head effigy jar. 1200–1600. Height 6 in. Temple Mound II, Blytheville, Arkansas. Museum of the American Indian, Heye Foundation, New York

37. Pottery water bottle with circular base. Blackware with incised decoration. Height 7·25 in. Carden Bottom, Yell County, Arkansas. Museum of the American Indian, Heye Foundation, New York

38. Stone pipe in the form of a warrior. 1200–1600. Height 9·75 in. Spiro Mound, Le Flore County, Oklahoma. Museum of the American Indian, Heye Foundation, New York

39. Stone figure of a seated woman. Height 15·5 in. Tumlin Mound, Barlow County, Georgia. Museum of the American Indian, Heye Foundation, New York

37

38   39

43

21, 22, 29 experts can identify the origin of a Great Pueblo pot by certain telltale signs of decoration, hardness, and general texture. Black-on-white decoration appears in many forms. On some bowls the black paint is applied in such a manner as to elicit a white design, as in a negative. On other pieces there are distinctive kinds of scrolls, hatching, and line work which make for regional variations. There are also variations in the shapes to be found. Polychrome bowls also begin to make their appearance, probably produced for trade, from the St John's region of Arizona. Some of the distinguished pottery styles from this era are: Sagi Black-on-White, Mesa Verde Black-on-White, Chaco Black-on-White, Tularosa Black-on-White, Mimbres **25** Black-on-White, and St John's Polychrome.

From tree ring datings and other evidence, we know that disaster struck the people of the Great Pueblo period. The great cities of Chaco Canyon, Mesa Verde, and the Kayenta area (to mention only the most famous) were abandoned by 1300. Why? Perhaps civil strife is one answer. Perhaps the incessant and dangerous marauding of the Athapaskans is another. More profoundly, however, we believe that a great drought must have been decisive. Between 1276 and 1300 the Southwest was struck by a lack of rainfall that must have been nothing short of catastrophic for these agriculturists. For almost 25 years these people had to endure a drought of unremitting severity. Since the Southwest was (and still is) undergoing a gradual process of aridization anyway, the difficulty of attempting to raise crops under such circumstances must have been close to impossible. Under these sorts of conditions, the prehistoric Southwesterners had to search out more secure sources of water. In doing so, they had to abandon the villages they had labored to build for so long.

Nonetheless, during a 200-year period of expansion (1100–1300), the Anasazi extended their culture over an area of unprecedented size.

Regressive Pueblo From approximately 1300 to the historic period of the establishment of Spanish influence in the American Southwest around 1600, the Pueblo peoples sought to establish themselves in regions of more secure water resources. They searched out such areas as the Rio Grande valley, the locale around present-day Zuni Pueblo, and the Hopi Pueblos region in order to relocate and build new lives.

As several experts have pointed out, in some respects this epoch can be considered as the real golden age for the Pueblo peoples since their culture, quite the opposite from deteriorating in this period of retrenchment, actually flourished and achieved new greatness. Pueblo architecture became more sophisticated with new developments in central courts and *kivas*.

With regard to pottery in particular, the Regressive Pueblo period is witness to new refinements, technological innovations, and artistic excellence. Mineral glaze paints and new types of polychromes come on the scene to replace declining black-on-white and corrugated forms. Regional variations are once again quite important. Some of the distinctive pottery styles of this epoch are: Pecos Polychrome, Sikyatki Poly-**31** chrome, Hawikuh Polychrome, Zuni Black-on-White,

Four-Mile Polychrome, and Gila Polychrome.

It is in the Regressive Pueblo period that we find evidence of a new ceremonial cult. From the ruins of such now deserted Regressive Pueblo villages as Awatovi (in the Hopi group) we find remains of mural paintings on the walls of *kivas*. These highly abstract and symbolic renderings of things like birds, masked dancers, and mythological beasts, suggest a new and highly developed religious form. J. O. Brew (in *Franciscan Awatovi*, 1949) believes these paintings are derived from influences eminating from the Tlaloc region of central Meso-America. He further argues that such paintings as these could be the harbingers of the more modern Katchina cult which is still active today. More will be said about the Katchina in the section on modern Southwestern Indians.

Be that as it may, with the closing of the Regressive Pueblo period in 1600 and the emergence of the Southwest into the historical era we end our discussion of prehistory in this fascinating region.

The Southeast

The second area of prehistoric interest is in that section of the United States we might designate as the Southeast. It includes a vast chunk of land extending from the Ohio River valley in the north to the Gulf of Mexico in the south, and from the Atlantic Ocean in the east to as far west as the Canadian River in Oklahoma. Generally speaking, however, the heartland area of this prehistoric culture lies in the landmass bounded by the Ohio and Mississippi Rivers and the Atlantic Ocean and Gulf of Mexico. Herein, a diverse group of people built mounds as early as 1000 BC and developed a material culture full of extraordinary beauty, particularly in the ceramic arts. Contrary to early belief, the prehistoric culture of the Southeast was not created by a single, homogeneous people, nor did these people suddenly and mysteriously 'disappear' from the pages of history. Their descendants continued to populate the Woodlands area into the time of white occupation, although the height of this culture was already past when the Spanish soldier of fortune, De Soto, landed in the American South in 1539.

As with the Southwest, there is considerable evidence to suggest that Mexican influence in this region was seminal. It is very possible—and even probable—that Meso-American culture was responsible, at least indirectly, for many of the developments which characterize this Southeastern civilization. Moreover, there may have been a very similar kind of mercantilistic system in this area not unlike the one which may have pertained in the Southwest. That a metropolis/hinterland relationship was likely in this region would give coherence to the pattern of development we witness for the Southeast. There is no doubt that the Southeast had many products desirable to an avaricious civilization in the Valley of Mexico, and in return they would receive numerous ideas and physical commodities from the metropolitan center. If anything, an inspection of the material culture of the American Southeast gives us cause to believe that this is even more true here than for the Southwest.

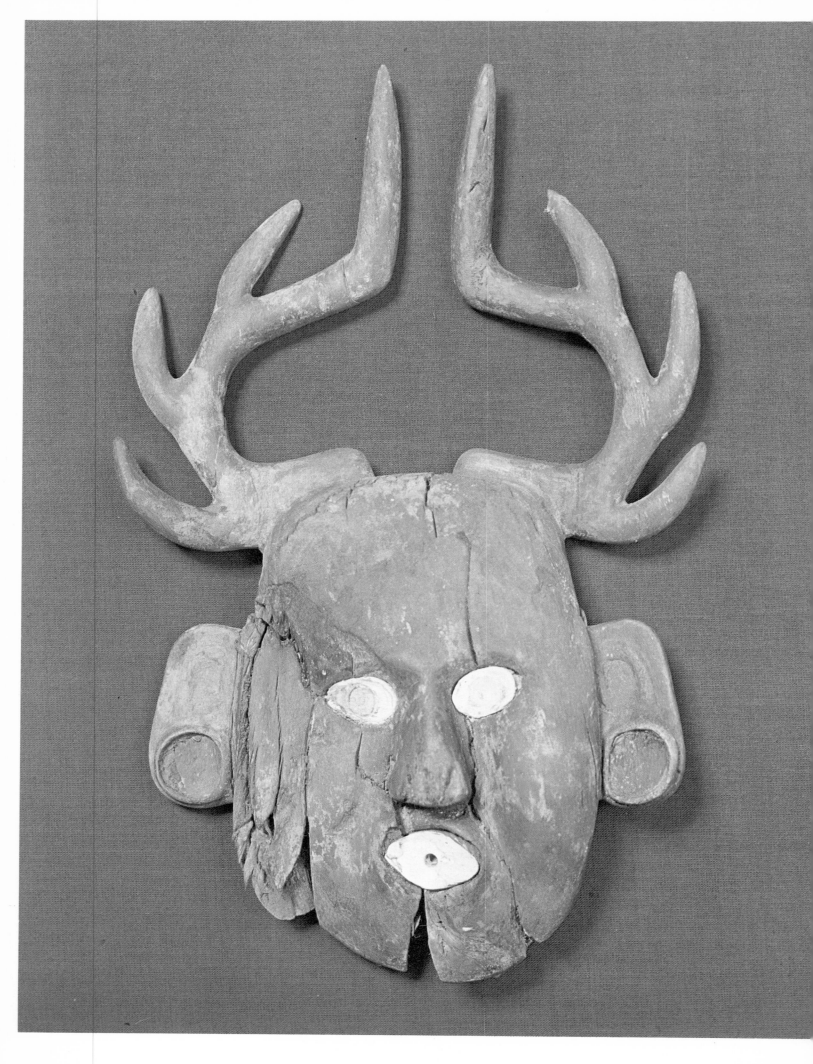

opposite 41. Wooden deer mask, inlaid with shell. Height 11·5 in. Temple Mound, Le Flore County, Oklahoma. Museum of the American Indian, Heye Foundation, New York

below 42. Embossed copper sheet showing human head. Height 9·5 in. Temple Mound, Le Flore County, Oklahoma. Museum of the American Indian, Heye Foundation, New York

As with our previous study, however, it would be improper to assume that Southeastern culture came into existence all at once and fully developed. On the contrary, there was a long period of development before the civilization of the Mississippian period came into full flower. Indeed, we can discern a number of distinct stages before the Moundbuilder culture came into being.

In the Southeast, as well as the Southwest, we can begin with the existence of a Paleo-Indian Tradition sometime around 8000 BC. Although no glacier ever penetrated into the Southeast, there was a great deal of rainfall that nourished a fairly thick forest cover. In such an environment, early hunters roamed seeking out big game animals. Evidence of Clovis Man has been found here in profusion just as it has in the Southwest.

After the last Wisconsin ice sheet had retreated, there was a new climate with changed environmental conditions. The people who lived during this period, around 6000 to 4000 BC, hunted the available smaller animals and supplemented their diet with shellfish, nuts, roots, and seeds. At first there were no dramatic differences between these people, who lived in what we call the Archaic Period, and the Paleo-Indians who came before them, except that there were certain technical advances and cultural refinements. With more tools and a more specialized social system, they were able to wrest a living from the environment and achieve a more varied culture.

Later on, however, they either developed or received (possibly from Mexico) the rudiments of what would lead to a sedentary mode of existence. Early forms of corn, squash, and beans were introduced from Mexico, and these innovations provided the basis for a more secure form of earning a living. The earliest dated pottery in North America is from the Southeast where by possibly 2000 BC it was a known craft. With the appearance of reliable containers, crops could be stored and further cultural developments were possible. With the establishment of true agriculture, the

47

knowledge of pottery, and the capacity for sedentary life, we can inspect the first important stage of pre-historic Southeastern civilization, the Woodland period.

The Woodland period

In this general stage of Southeastern development, we encounter the first two cultures which are fundamental to defining the Southeast itself: the Adena and Hopewell lifeways. It is with them that we first encounter the identifying hallmark of Southeastern culture: the building of mounds to commemorate the dead and to carry on ceremonial and religious functions. The Southeast did not duplicate the feat of Southwestern people by building great cities of stone. For their part, it is the construction of great mounds that must stand as their prime architectural contribution to the culture of North American prehistory. These mounds can be classified into three basic categories: human burial, effigy, and temple mounds. The Adena and Hopewell peoples built the Indian burial and effigy-type mounds; the Mississippi culture was responsible for the temple mounds.

In the valley of the Ohio River grew up an early culture to which we have given the name Adena. From approximately 1000 BC to about AD 200, the Adena Indians built numerous burial mounds for their dead. While they were very simple at first, the later Adena people were capable of building circular earthworks and large, elaborately constructed mounds. In such earthworks they buried their dead with incredibly rich offerings. Objects interred with the dead would include art works of mica and copper, incised pottery, pearl beads, engraved tablets, textiles, and various pieces of personal ornamentation. Sometimes tubular stone smoking pipes and polished stone axes would also accompany the burial in a mound. This extraordinary care taken in the interment of deceased persons indicates that the Adena people, as were the others who came after them, were preoccupied with (and even obsessed by) the spectre of death.

The importance of mounds built for the dead in this culture has prompted archaeologists to suggest that there was a death cult amongst these people. In other words, it would appear that death and rituals surrounding the dead were a central theme in the Adena's cultural apparatus. While many peoples over the earth have expressed an interest in the issue of life after death, it seems that the Southeastern people put that question very near the center of their concerns.

While the Adena people had some type of agriculture in the very late years of their existence, for the most part they depended on hunting and gathering for their food. They lived in circular houses which were roofed over with thatch or bark and had walls of woven saplings that were bound to posts. While simple in many ways, the contributions of this culture were important for later Hopewellian developments. Generally speaking, the Adena are said to occupy the Early Woodland period of cultural evolution.

Around 100 BC, the Hopewell arose in the Ohio valley region with a culture that was eventually to supplant the earlier Adena phase. The exact nature of the relationship between the Adena and Hopewell peoples has not yet been resolved. What we do know is that the Hopewellians took many Adena ideas and technological innovations in order to amplify them further. They constructed large conical or dome-shaped burial mounds (some 30 feet or more in height and 200 feet in circumference) which dotted the central Mississippi and Illinois River valleys. In addition to burial mounds, they also contructed effigy mounds in the shape of serpents, animals, and so on.

In terms of Hopewell economic and social culture, great advances were made over previous Adena forms. The Hopewellians were agriculturists who raised corn, squash, beans, and tobacco, while living in semi-permanent villages set apart from the ceremonial centers. Their dwellings were very likely dome-roofed wigwams covered with skins, mats, or sheets of bark. What is also noteworthy about their culture is the elaborate system of trade and communications which they worked out. It is clear that the Hopewellians had a network of trade relations that stretched over almost the entire continent. From different regions they obtained a number of varied materials with which to fashion art objects for interment with the dead.

The production of articles for inclusion in burials was a major stimulus for the development of extraordinary arts and crafts. As Alvin M. Josephy, Jr, has expressed it in *The Indian Heritage of America*, their material culture was impressive:

'. . . articles of all kinds and for many uses were produced in profusion and with artistic excellence. Tools were made of copper, stone, bone, and antler. Ornaments, including bead necklaces, arm bands, pendants, and ear and breast decorative pieces, were fashioned from metal, shell, bone and stone. Fine pottery of several styles, including some of the best made at any time by Indians in the Northeast, was produced; spoons and other utensils were made of various materials, including shells; cloth was woven with thread made from the soft inner bark of certain trees; and stone bowls of tobacco pipes were sculptured beautifully in the form of humans and animals. Artistic abilities reached a climax in the making of effigy forms of copper and mica, the sculpturing in stone and bone, and the engraving on bone, shell, and wood. Musical instruments, including panpipes, various types of rattles, and, probably, drums, were also made.'

Thus it was a period of great creativity in the arts and progress in material culture.

The social system that accompanied this outward expression must have been highly differentiated. We believe that they had a strong class structure in which there was a distinct division of labor. At the top there must have been a class of nobles with hereditary rank and privileges. No doubt they were aided by a strong religious system in which there were priests who must have had considerable power. Perhaps political and spiritual power were united in one entity. Beneath those exalted levels there would be the common people who provided the specialized skills of metalworkers, artists, traders, and so on.

The Hopewell culture also expanded beyond the conventional bounds of the American Southeast. Its influence—which might have included colonizers as well—moved in a northeasterly, northern, and western direction. Evidence of the Hopewell development is commonly found in the Northeast seaboard area of the United States, the Great Lakes region, and even out upon the Plains. It goes without saying that these outposts of the Hopewell culture were subject to peculiar local conditions but their relationship to the Hopewellian heartland is nonetheless obvious.

Around 500 or 700 however, the Hopewell culture faded and ultimately gave way to other developments taking place further south. Nevertheless, these people had made a significant contribution to the prehistoric civilizations east of the Mississippi.

The Mississippian period

With the emergence of the third major cultural force in the prehistory of the Southeast, the Mississippi, we find a people who constructed the great temple mounds that so attracted the imagination of early historians. Some of these early chroniclers thought that the builders of such mounds must have been a race of people who mysteriously disappeared from the face of the earth after finishing their gargantuan tasks. We now know that the descendants of these people in the Southeast—the Natchez, Chickasaw, Chocktaw, Cherokee, and others—were simply the•less prepossessing inheritors of a distinguished culture that was well into decline by the 1540s.

The Mississippian culture arose around 700 and thrived until 1400. This whole society was made possible by a strong agricultural base that may have been deeply indebted to Mexico. There is evidence, certainly, that this region was heavily influenced by the Huastec area of northeastern Mexico. Be that as it may, the Mississippians built sizeable towns close to the formidable mounds they constructed, on the top of which they placed temples. The mounds were flat-topped, and the buildings usually thatch-roofed rectangular structures on which effigies of birds were sometimes placed. One chronicler of De Soto, after observing a temple in the province of Cofachiqui in the 1539–41 period, wrote the following commentary:

'Now this temple was large, being more than a hundred feet in length and forty in width. Its walls were high . . . and its roof was also very lofty and drafty . . . Over the roof of the temple many large and small shells of different marine animals had been arranged . . . These shells had been placed with the inside out so as to show their greatest luster, and they included many conch shells of strange magnificence. Between them, spaces had been left . . . and in these spaces were large strands (some of pearls and some of seed pearls) half a fathom in length which hung from the roof and descended in a graduated manner so that where some left off others began. The temple was covered on the outside with all these things, and they made a splendid sight in the brilliance of the sun.'

After the 10th century, the Mississippian culture spread rapidly through most of the Southeast and even as far west as present-day Oklahoma. Several important sites bear witness to the significance of the Mississippian phenomenon: Ocmulgee on central Georgia's Macon Plateau; Moundville on Alabama's Black Warrior River; the Angel site in southwestern Indiana; Aztalan in Wisconsin; Spiro in eastern Oklahoma; and Etowah in Georgia.

These people, too, were preoccupied with the fact of death in human existence. Like the Adena and Hopewell stages that had preceded them, some areas of the temple-mound civilization definitely embraced a complex of human activities which are termed the 'Southern Cult', or what is also known as the 'Southern Death Cult' or 'Buzzard Cult.' The final development of this cultural orientation may have been influenced, as the initial stages of it in the Adena and Hopewell forms had been influenced, by new ideas from Mexico. Whatever might be the case, here, too, a vast array of superlative arts and crafts was produced for interment with the dead. Native-mined copper, for example, was hammered into ornate plaques, ear spools, head- **42** dresses, and so on. Shells, imported from the Gulf Coast, were elaborately engraved with intricate sym- **16** bolic designs. Pottery of all kinds, polished stonework, **39** sculptured likenesses of animals, and other items were the kind of arts brought to new heights during this period.

The case of the Spiro Mound is instructive for our purposes since several objects from that site are illustrated here. Although the mound was tragically looted in 1933–35 by a group of pot hunters calling themselves the Pocola Mining Company, several of the more important items have been retrieved and are available for study. Mr and Mrs Henry W. Hamilton of the Missouri Archaeological Society have catalogued the contents of the mound insofar as they were able to and have produced the following astonishing record: some 120 or more pipes (23 of which are effigies in **38** animal or human form); 11 human figures carved of cedar; more than 40 cedar masks; 50 chipped maces; and nearly 200 conch shells which were engraved **33** with intricate mythological scenes and religious motifs.

While some of the pottery from this period is of an effigy type, in that it attempts to portray some kind of animal or human form, it is clear that the symbolic aspects of such effigy work are far more important than the naturalistic aspects. Indeed, it would be hard to consider much of this effigy modeling as realistic in any Western sense of the word. The rest of the ceramics from this period, whether painted or incised, show at a glance a strong proclivity towards abstract and symbolic design. The pottery output of this period is notable for its excellence and can take its place beside the other arts being produced at this time.

Some of the ceramics shown here, particularly those from the Arkansas-Tennessee-Missouri States region **34, 35, 36, 37** are from the last stages of the Mississippian culture and transitional into the historic period. Many of them would date roughly from 1400 to 1700.

While the doom of the Mississippi culture was sealed with the advent of the Spanish, it is nonetheless true that the decline of this civilization had already set in before the white man came to North American shores. While Natchez chiefs fascinated early explorers with demonstrations of fragments of this dying culture—such as their own elaborate lifestyle and still-practised rituals of their ceremonial life—it is clear that the Temple Mound stage of Southeast civilization had come or was coming to a predictable end. Whether or not there would have been a subsequent and higher stage of this culture is something we shall never know.

The Southwest

Prehistory comes to an end in the American Southwest with the entry of Francisco Vasquez de Coronado and his party in 1540. With the extension of Spanish greed into this territory, the Southwestern Indians came into contact with the white man and, hence, knowledge of native customs is no longer necessarily in the hands of archaeologists. In our examination of the cultures of this region of the United States, including primarily the states of Arizona and New Mexico, we will classify these peoples into three primary categories: the Athapaskan Raiders, the Pueblo Agriculturists, and the Desert People.

Coronado came north seeking gold. For years rumors had been circulating in Mexico about the possibility of the existence of fabulous wealth in the north. Since fiction accumulated upon fiction, the story soon gained credence that there were seven cities of solid gold located beyond the Sonoran desert awaiting only the ruthless hand of a conqueror from the Valley of Mexico. These fabled metropolises of treasure became known as 'the Seven Cities of Cibola.' Supposedly, these seven cities were built out of solid gold with streets and other civic accoutrements similarly constructed. All that was needed, it was said, was for a conquistadore of the stature of Cortez or Pizarro to snap up such prizes.

The rumors were fed when two refugees from a wrecked exploring party, a Catholic priest named Fray Marcos and a black slave named Esteben, actually claimed to have been in the proximity of the Seven Cities of Cibola while wandering around in the north. Esteben stated that he had truly viewed one of the cities from the top of a nearby hill and seen its golden spires glittering in the sun. This drove the Spaniards into a frenzy of desire for easy booty, and ultimately an expedition under the command of Coronado was organized in order to loot and pillage these ripe victims. To make a long story short, there were, of course, no cities of gold and no booty to be had. Instead, Coronado's party met up with only poor Puebloan villagers in the Regressive Period of Puebloan culture.

It is fairly sure that the villages which Coronado visited during his expedition were several in number: some of the Pueblos located in the present vicinity of Zuni which were then known as Hawikuh and Acoma, and the Rio Grande Pueblos like Pecos. Discouraged and disheartened after a period of wandering about and terrorizing the natives, a journey which took him out onto the Plains, he and his party returned to Mexico empty-handed. Nonetheless, parties of settlers and government administrators arrived not too long afterwards in order to establish Spanish colonies in this region of New Spain.

In the 1600s the Spanish established a strong and viable colonial domain in northern New Spain, particularly in what is now the state of New Mexico. They attempted a thorough subjugation of the Pueblo peoples along the Rio Grande and endeavored to do the same for the more devious Navajo and Apache. Apart from economic and political domination, the Spaniards sought to consolidate their rule over the native peoples by converting them, peaceably if possible or by force if necessary, to the Catholic faith of the Europeans. The yoke of New Spain was a harsh one for the Puebloan people to bear. Not only were traditional freedoms a thing of the past but now the Puebloans had to endure the brunt of economic exploitation. Priests came into their village and both prohibited and ridiculed their age-old faiths and customs. Since Catholic missionaries had Spanish military muscle to back them up, the people lived under a constant terror that is the lot of any harshly oppressed humanity.

Such domination was not to be born without protest, however. One Rio Grande medicine man, or *Cacique*, by the name of Pope, resolved that something had to be done to remove the stern rule of the Spaniards. After much deliberation, he and other fellow conspirators decided that a concerted uprising was the only answer to their dilemma. That is exactly what happened in the Pueblo Revolt of 1680. Pope arranged with the leadership of all the Pueblo villages that at a pre-arranged time they would rise up in unison and throw off the yoke of their oppressor. Priests would be killed, the Catholic faith exterminated as an alien influence, settlers chased off ancestral lands, and the colonial leadership would be exiled from native territory. The attack was successful and Santa Fe was hurriedly abandoned by fleeing Spaniards who returned to the relative safety of Mexico. The plotters made good their plan to expunge Spanish influences in the area.

The Hopi, more physically isolated than the other Puebloan peoples, went to considerable lengths in their attempt to eradicate Spanish influence. For example, at the Pueblo of Oraibi in 1680 the Indians killed the priests and destroyed the mission church. They got rid of the priests' bodies by throwing them over the mesa cliff. When, in 1700, after the Spanish had returned to reconquer their territories and the easternmost Hopi Pueblo of Awatovi had once again accepted Catholic missionaries, the other Hopi villages turned against this Pueblo with unprecedented fury.

*43. A Hopi girl. Her elaborate hairstyle denotes her
unmarried state. Photograph by Edward S. Curtis*

They killed all of the males above a certain age, took the women and children and redistributed them amongst the other villages, and abandoned Awatovi.

The ferocity of Hopi resistance to Spanish influence during and after the Revolt of 1680 tended to discourage any efforts to re-establish Spanish presence in the area. No doubt the Hopis were helped in their policy by the fact that between them and the Spanish in New Mexico were the fierce Navajo. The constant warfare between the Spanish and Navajo peoples virtually precluded the possibility of renewed Spanish colonization in the case of the Hopi.

In 1692, however, the Spaniards re-entered the Southwest territory and this time they came to stay. The Rio Grande Puebloan peoples were not so fortunate as their western counterparts in avoiding the Spanish yoke. These Puebloan peoples had to adopt a policy of passive resistance to white authority; a policy which they still adhere to today. Unable to resist Spanish domination with force, these Indian people adopted a line of ostensible cooperation but hidden opposition. One of their principal weapons was secrecy. It became a policy of these tribes not to divulge important knowledge about themselves to anyone outside the culture. The tribe would attempt to keep secret as much information as was possible about all manner of Indian beliefs and practices. Perhaps if the white man did not know the fundamental (or superficial) truths about the Indian people, he would find it difficult if not impossible to exercise control. It might even be possible for Indians to pretend to go along with the white man's wishes—or to actually conform on non-essential issues—in order to deflect the real force of the conqueror.

The Indian discovered that he might be able to prevent some of the worst excesses of white power by such a form of passive resistance. While it was true nonetheless that he could not guide and direct his own destiny in his own land anymore, the power of white authority might be minimized by secrecy and other forms of passive non-compliance. Sometimes Indians would pretend not to understand white demands in order to avoid carrying them out. At other times they might feign inability and helplessness in order to ward off the policies of white governments. The Indian understood the principle that if someone else is to dominate you, he must secure your active compliance at least in certain ways in order to do so. While non-compliance and passive resistance would not succeed in freeing you, at least such behavior would minimize the amount of control.

There is no doubt that the Indians of the Southwest have maintained more of their original and historic culture than other native peoples in North America. One of the key reasons for this is, no doubt, the fact that the white man considered much of their land undesirable and therefore let them alone to eke out a living upon it. That the whites did not covet the land of the Southwestern peoples as much as in the east or on the Great Plains was a saving grace for these tribes. Also important, however, were the effective forms of passive resistance such as is found in the

44. The blanket-weaver, Navajo. Photograph by Edward S. Curtis

principle of secrecy. The Hopis, for example, banned cameras from their mesas shortly after the turn of the century, and no white people are allowed to prowl around their underground ceremonial chambers or *kivas*.

It goes without saying that the Southwest Indians were not the only native peoples in North America to adopt such lines of opposition. Their good fortune was to be able to organize strategies of passive resistance and to live in an area not greatly desired by white greed.

Let us briefly survey each of the three major tribal traditions in the contemporary Southwest: the Athapaskan Raiders, the Pueblo Agriculturists, and the People of the Desert.

The Athapaskan Raiders

As we have already intimated, it is very likely that Indians from the MacKenzie regions of Canada and Alaska may have found their way down to the Southwest region from the period AD 1100 to 1300. These northern Athapaskan people were ancestors of the modern Navajo and Apache Indians. Today the Navajo live on a giant reservation around the Four Corners area of Arizona, Utah, New Mexico, and Colorado, although the biggest chunk of their land is located in the first named state. It occupies a land size as large as the combined states of Vermont, New Hampshire, Massachusetts, Connecticut, and Rhode Island. The Apaches are sprinkled around on reservations in both Arizona and New Mexico bearing the names White Mountain, Mescalero, Jicarilla, and San Carlos.

In the early days these two tribes ranged over the entire area of the Southwest. They were hunters, gatherers, and, most importantly to the sedentary Puebloan peoples, raiders. It was their habit to swoop down upon the hapless Pueblo Indians at appropriate times, especially after the harvest was in, in order to steal women, haul away food stuffs, and loot whatever treasures they could find in the villages. While there were no doubt periods of truce between certain of the raiders and some of the Pueblos, the history of their relations is one of more or less unremitting warfare. The late and distinguished archaeologist, Adolf A. Bandelier, wrote an affecting fictional tale of what life must have been like for Pueblo peoples subject to such harassment, in his famous book, *The Delight Makers*.

When the Spaniards and other white men came, the Navajo and Apache added them to their list of blood enemies. In fact, there was particularly bitter enmity between these Athapaskan Indians and the Spaniards and Mexicans. The Spanish-speaking peoples would often seize these Athapaskans at any available opportunity and impress them into slavery, a singularly odious fate for any of these raider people. As a result, the two peoples raided each other unmercifully.

The Navajo were a bit different from their Apache cousins, though. The former have demonstrated in history an uncanny ability to take ideas and things from other people and utilize them effectively within their own cultural context. In other words, they are capable of taking contributions from other cultures and running with them to destinations of the Navajo's own choosing. The Navajo are a brilliantly eclectic people who know how to adopt the possessions and notions of others without losing the sense of 'Navajo-izing' it and making it their own.

One extraordinary example of this principle is the Navajo development of weaving. When the Spanish brought sheep to the Southwest after 1600, they introduced something totally new to the nomadic Navajo. While the Navajo enjoyed sheep as food, it also became clear that the wool was valuable as an additional resource. In their raiding of Pueblo villages, it was common practice for Navajo men to seize Pueblo women if and when possible in order to make wives of them. These women, as we already know, possessed the knowledge of the weaving of textiles from their experience with cotton. With the advent of sheep into Navajo life, the Pueblo women taught Navajo women how to weave and it was sheep's wool that became the textile fiber in this case. While the Navajo have a legend that it was Spider Woman who taught them how to weave, the truth is much more prosaic.

The genius of Navajo imagination came to the fore when Spanish sheep were combined with Pueblo technology in order to suggest the possibility of a hybrid textile for the Navajos. The Dineh (the Navajo's name for themselves) took these elements and made them into something unique and distinctively Navajo. Out of this cross-fertilization came Navajo rugs which today are world famous. The Navajo realized that the keeping of sheep would necessitate certain changes in their style of life, from a totally footloose tribe to nomadic sheepherders, but they accomplished the transition with grace and minimal cultural damage. As early as 1700 they were producing textiles of note. It was not long before the Navajos were producing textiles in a variety of forms such as saddle blankets, **45** shoulder blankets, and women's dresses.

The classic period of Navajo weaving is usually dated from 1850 to around 1875. During this period, the Navajos produced textiles of unusual excellence and quality: they were tightly woven, and the aesthetic virtues of these pieces are unquestioned. Women's dresses (actually executed in a Puebloan style) and the so-called Chief's Blanket are excellent examples of the weaving of this period. Early Navajo design shows a desire for tasteful simplicity and the economical use of color. Design motifs are rather basic and tend to be repeated in layers on the blanket. Colors are never garish or vulgar but blended and rich. During this time span the Navajo weavers (always women) obtained Bayeta cloth from Mexico and unraveled it in order to incorporate the yarn into their own rugs. The rich red of Bayeta is a hallmark of the best weaving of this era. It is also true that in the classic period the Navajos utilized natural vegetable dyes for many of their colors. These pale shades of pastel hues gave Navajo blankets a softspoken demeanor that is most attractive.

The classic period was not destined to last, however. The Navajos had been giving Anglo settlers in the Southwest a very difficult time of it, just as they had made life miserable for the Spaniards and Mexicans. Their raiding patterns by the 1860s were causing much anxiety amongst federal authorities who already had their hands full with the Civil War. Ever since the Americans took possession of the Southwest from the Mexicans in 1848, they had had trouble with the

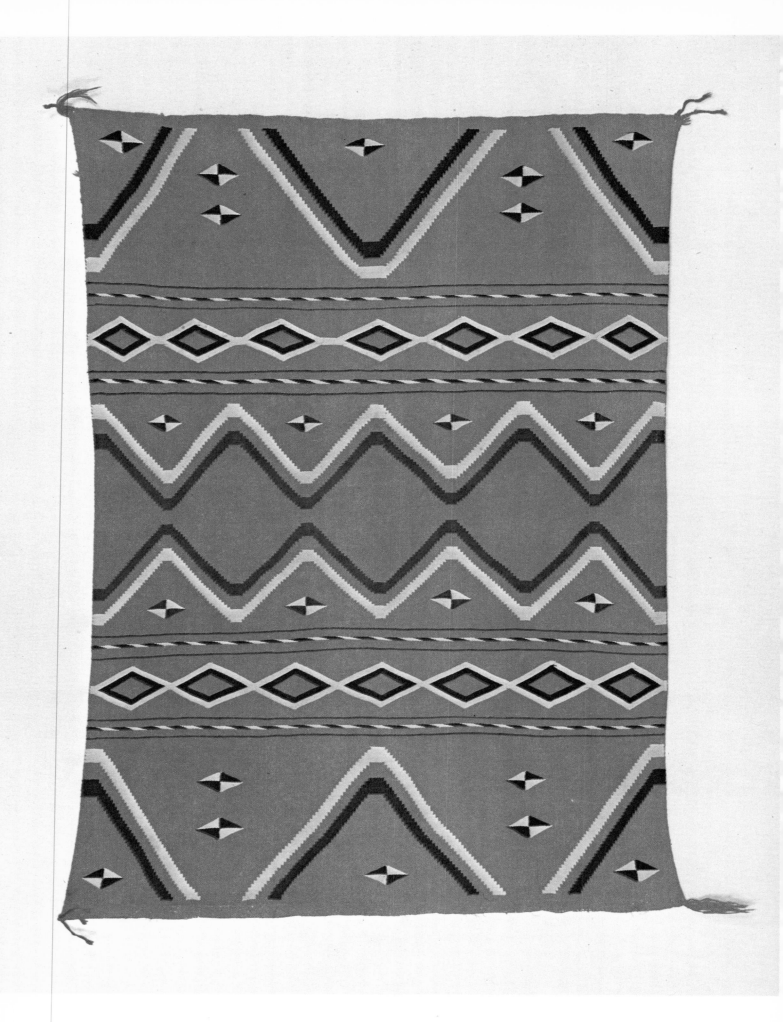

*45. Blanket. 40 × 58 in. Navajo, New Mexico. Museum of the
American Indian, Heye Foundation, New York*

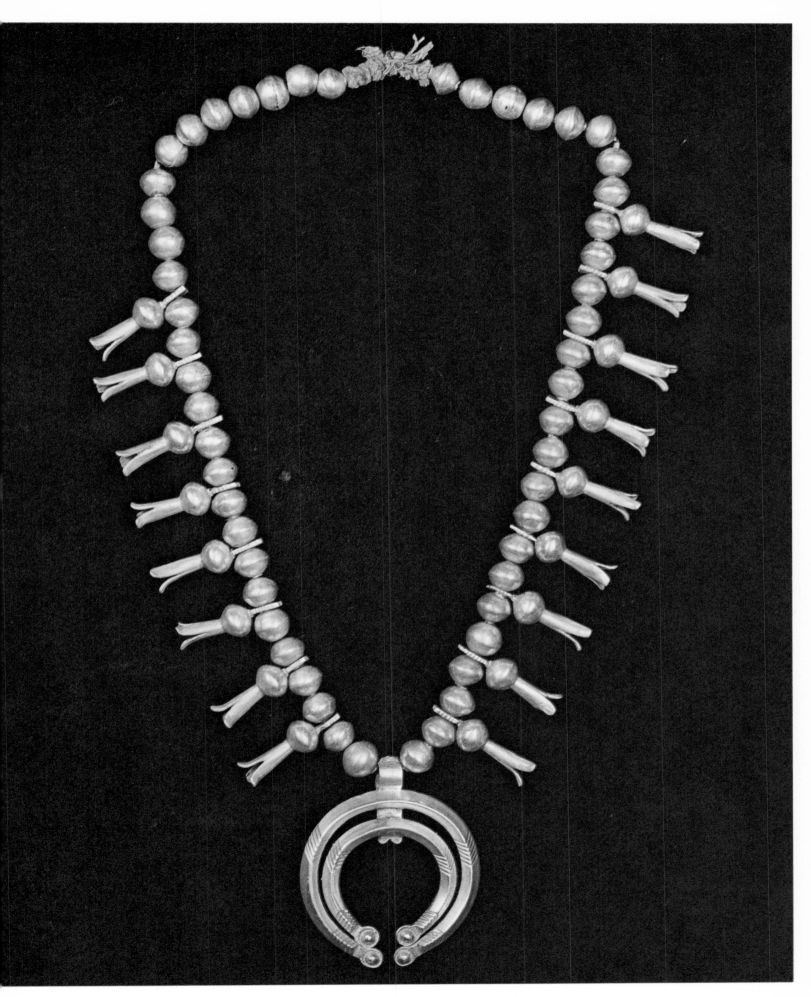

46. Silver squash blossom necklace. Length 12·5 in. Navajo,
New Mexico. Museum of the American Indian, Heye
Foundation, New York

47. Pima Ki. The traditional round, earth dwelling of the Piman tribes who live in Arizona. The hut was usually some 15 feet in diameter. Photograph by Edward S. Curtis.

48. *Teec Nos Pos outline rug. Navajo. Red Mesa Trading*
Post, Arizona

49. Vegetable dye rug. Navajo. Wide Ruins Trading Post,
Arizona

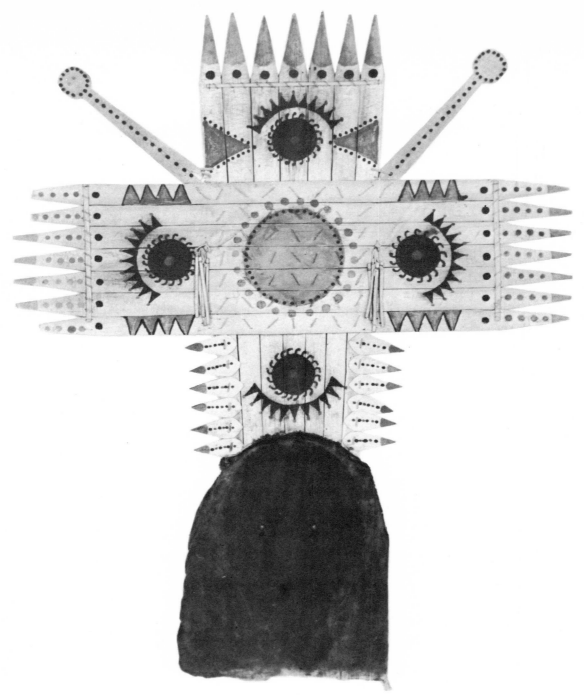

*50. Devil Dance mask. San Carlos Apache, Arizona. Museum
of the American Indian, Heye Foundation, New York*

Navajos and Apaches. In 1863 the United States government decided it had put up long enough with Navajo independence and ordered Kit Carson to round up all the Dineh he could find in order to deport them from their homeland.

By 1864 most of the Navajos had been rounded up and sent off to exile. In 1866 even the great Navajo chief, Manuelito, was forced to surrender and, along with other Navajos, required to take the 'long walk' to an abominable locale in eastern New Mexico named Basque Redondo. It was a terrible place and the Navajo perished in great numbers from the bad water and lack of food. To all intents and purposes it was a concentration camp. After four years of incarceration in this economically unviable location, it became evident to most that the Navajo would either have to be allowed to go home or they would perish. Thus, in 1868, the Navajo signed a treaty pledging themselves to perpetual peace with the white man in return for a

portion of their ancestral lands as a reservation.

With great relief, the Dineh returned to their beloved country of canyons, mesas, deserts, and plateaux. Here they attempted to resume as much of their previous life as they could. They developed their herds of sheep and became a more pastoral people who tended flocks and practised a limited amount of agriculture. As we have pointed out before, however, the Navajo are a tough and extraordinarily adaptable people who know how to confront life and new realities without losing their sense of who they are.

In the new reservation period, many white traders moved onto the Navajo land in order to set up trading posts. Licensed by the federal government, they sold the Navajo groceries and other commodities of the white men in return for wool, rugs, jewelry, and other produce. Inevitably, Navajo weaving began to change in response to these new developments. The classic period of Navajo textiles was to pass away and yield to a more decadent epoch of weaving. While some very fine rugs were produced in the time span from 1880 to around 1930, there were increasing tendencies towards garishness in color, crudeness in the weaving and a lack of refinement in general. Many traders paid the women for their rugs by the pound instead of by the quality of weaving or the tastefulness in design. Consequently, many of the rugs produced in this era for the eastern market and tourist trade were of very dubious worth. Some of the better products of this period are rugs utilizing Germantown yarn which was almost as rich in its red as the earlier Bayeta (by this time unavailable). As with most North American Indian arts and crafts, the 1880 to 1930 era was particularly discouraging, both in terms of the quantity of output and the quality of that production.

In the 1930s, though, there was renewed interest in improving and encouraging the weaving of fine quality Navajo rugs. Under John Collier, the Bureau of Indian Affairs began to undertake an active program to improve Dineh weaving. In addition to government efforts, many of the more concerned traders on the reservation, like Sally and Bill Lippincott at the Wide Ruins Trading Post, engaged in more private initiatives to help their weavers do better and receive more money for doing so. Earlier in the century, L. H. 'Cozy' McSparron worked hard with his weavers in order to thwart the degenerate tendencies in Navajo textiles. The sum of these efforts resulted in a general upgrading of Navajo work and the emergence of these textiles as a major art form in the mid 20th century. Income was also improved for the weaver, although not nearly so much as for the middleman trader and retailer.

Today it can be said that the quality of Navajo weaving has never been higher. At the same time, however, it can also be pointed out that the quantity of rugs produced is going down every year. The average age of the excellent weavers is very high and few of the younger women seem attracted to this vocation—and understandably so since the work is difficult and the remuneration is still not adequate for the weaver. The Navajo rug remains an art form that is thoroughly Dineh: the Navajos tend their own flocks; sheer their own sheep; wash the wool and card it; spin and dye the yarn; and finally the woman weaves her yarn into a rug. There is never anything like a pattern board since the weaver has the design only in her own mind. Thus, no two Navajo rugs are ever alike; each one is a unique and distinctive piece of weaving.

On the reservation at present, there are general regions where some generic pattern types prevail; that is to say there is no one kind of Navajo rug which is produced everywhere. Also, while every single Navajo rug is unique in that it is never duplicated exactly, there are different areas of the Navajo reservation where certain styles of designs, weaving traditions, and color schemas do prevail in a very general sense.

The most important centers of contemporary Navajo weaving may be identified in the list below. Usually it is a prominent trading post in a particular area that gives to this regional style of weaving its generic name.

Two Gray Hills Beyond a doubt the most popular and universally esteemed rugs come from this area. They are invariably expertly woven with finely spun yarn. Intricate geometric patterns are executed utilizing the natural colors of wool—brown, white, gray and black (aniline reinforced).

Tuba City Here a rug known as the 'storm pattern' design is produced. It usually features a center box-shape with four lightning symbols connecting smaller squares in the corners of the rug. Black, white, gray, and red are the common colors.

Teec Nos Pos In the Four Corners area is a rug center **48** where all patterns, usually in geometric form, are outlined in another color. Aniline dyes are frequently used in these rugs to produce a vivid effect. It is said that the inspiration for the complicated designs of these rugs came from photos of Persian rugs which were shown to Navajo women around the turn of the century. The quality of the weaving is usually quite fine.

Shiprock This is the region where most of the Yei and sandpainting tapestries originate. The Yei design consists of narrow, elongated figures which represent supernatural beings. The sandpainting rugs are often replicas of designs found in the healing ceremonies of Navajo medicine men. Neither rug, however, possesses an intrinsic religious importance to the Navajos.

Crystal This is a region where the revival of vegetable dyes in the coloring of wool was pioneered. Insofar as many of these rugs approximate to the old styles, designs tend to be simple; bands with wavy lines predominate. Colors tend to be brown, yellow, rust, green, and black.

Wide Ruins/Pine Springs Another center of the revival of traditional weaving, rugs from this locale tend to be **49** very well woven in soft pastel hues. Designs from this area, as at Crystal, are simple, traditional motifs.

Ganado From this historic trading post, operated in the early days by Lorenzo Hubbell, traditional and distinguished red-black-white-gray rugs are produced. The very rich and deep red of these rugs has made them highly valued by almost any fancier of Navajo weaving. It can be said that for most people, these are the quintissential forms and designs of Navajo rugs.

Weaving is not the only art of the modern Navajo. They are equally famed as a people for their exquisite craftsmanship in silver and turquoise jewelry. We do not think the Navajo came into contact with metal-working as a craft until around 1850. Indeed, it was not until after the Basque Redondo experience that some Navajo men began to learn from and copy Mexican silversmithing techniques. Examples of the first bracelets and earrings are from the 1870 period. At first the Navajo used American silver dollars for their material, but when the defacing of US currency was prohibited they took to Mexican pesos. Around 1900 the Navajo began to use silver in great quantities in order to produce jewelry for the tourist trade. While the Navajos do turn out a great many items for their own use, the major sector of consumption has always been the white man.

Navajo silversmithing can be distinguished from the work of the Zuni and Hopi peoples. Navajo work tends to be more massive in its overall character. The design conception of Dineh silversmiths tends towards simplicity and clean-lined elegance. When turquoise stones are used, they tend to be fairly sizeable and more **52, 52** sparingly applied. Whereas the Zuni love to use multicolored stones in intricate mosaics of inlay work, the Navajo incline to rely more substantially on silver. Turquoise or coral stones are utilized in order to set off an essentially silver oriented masterpiece.

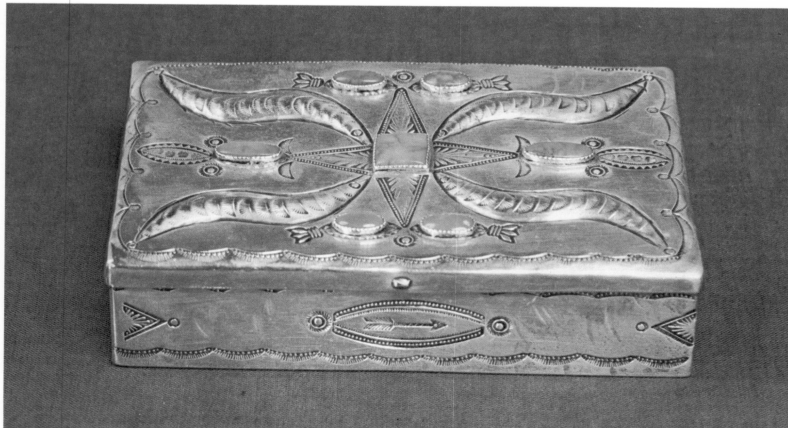

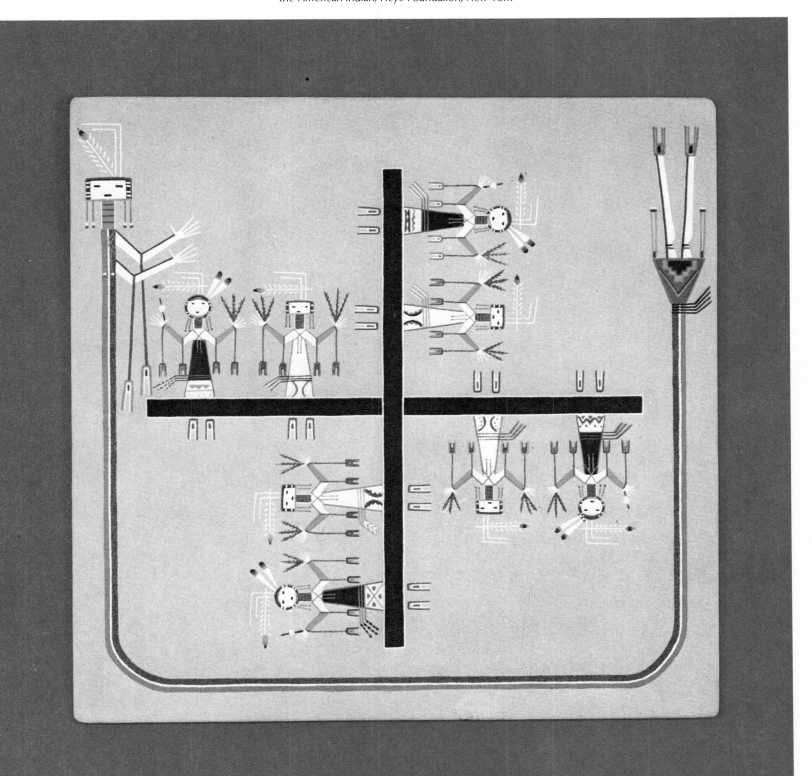

In terms of techniques, both hammered and sand-cast jewelry is made. In the first instance, the silver is hammered into a thin layer for cutting, filing, or stamping. In the second case of sandcasting, a soft rock is carved in the shape of the desired design. Then melted silver is poured into this rock and it serves as a mold. After the silver is removed from the mold, it is filed, polished and finished. With an array of only very simple tools, Navajo silversmiths have produced exceedingly **46** beautiful squash-blossom necklaces, bracelets, rings, and other ornamental items.

A final category of Navajo artistry which we will want to consider is their very impressive sandpainting. In a very profound sense, though, this is not art at all but a part of a serious ceremonial process. Sandpaintings are employed within the context of curing ceremonies and are executed either by medicine men or by their apprentices.

As we have already learned, the Indians as a people have a tendency to view the universe as a complete entity. All parts of the universe, each with its power for good and evil, are inextricably interrelated and contribute to the overall harmony of eternal being. The Navajo themselves give explicit endorsement to this conception of existence. Theirs is a devoutly religious and spiritual view of life and its meaning. When someone becomes ill, therefore, it is thought that the individual has left (or become out of phase with) the harmony of the universe. The purpose of curing, then, is to restore the human being to a previous state of harmony and being at one with all parts of creation and the universe.

It is the medicine man's function to come to the *hogan* (dwelling) of his patient and hold a 'chant' for the restoration of harmony. A chant, or 'sing' as it is sometimes referred to, is a complicated series of ceremonies which can last from one night to nine. During this period of time, the medicine man will use chants, songs, prayers, dances, prayer sticks, herbs, emetics, sweat baths (for purification), and sandpaintings. It is also common for the friends, neighbors, and relatives of the patient to gather round his *hogan* for this period in order to reassure him that he is not alone but an integral part of a whole community. To demonstrate this they might sing, dance, chant, and hold various sorts of social activities.

In the *hogan* the medicine man and his assistant (or assistants) will take crushed minerals and charcoal in order to 'paint' a sacred sandpainting on the dirt floor. When completed, the patient sits in the midst of the sandpainting in order to absorb the beauty and the essence of its meaning. Portions of the sandpainting that relate to the patient's specific illness are placed on his body. Later on, the sandpainting is ceremonially destroyed and buried lest it bring evil to some other person.

53 Very recently, some sandpaintings have been preserved on plyboard backgrounds and sold as an art form. (A viscous substance is mixed with the sand in order to fix it to the wood.) The designs are changed in such a way as to remove their religious significance, so that they might be treated as art rather than a part of a ceremonial process.

opposite 55. Antelope headdress decorated with paint, fur, hair and trade cloth. About 1900. Length 25 in. Chiricahua Apache, Arizona. Museum of the American Indian, Heye Foundation, New York

above 56. Painted skin used as a medicine shirt. Chiricahua Apache, Arizona. Museum of the American Indian, Heye Foundation, New York

below 57. Carved red ware 'wedding jar' with Avanyu design, by Margaret Tafoya. Height 13 in. San Ildefonso Pueblo, New Mexico. Museum of the American Indian, Heye Foundation, New York

below 59. Polychrome pottery bowl with fluted rim. About 1900. Height 13 in. Acoma Pueblo, New Mexico. Museum of the American Indian, Heye Foundation, New York

bottom 60. Jar made by Nampeyo, yellow ware with red and black painted decoration. Height 8·5 in. Hopi Pueblo, First Mesa. Museum of the American Indian, Heye Foundation, New York

opposite 61. Masau'u Katchina doll. Height 18 in. Hopi Pueblo, Arizona. Museum of the American Indian, Heye Foundation, New York

The mysticism and poetic spirit of the Navajo are very much in evidence in these healing ceremonies. Their chants are impressive paeans to the beauty of nature and the mystery of all creation:

With your moccasins of dark cloud, come to us!
With your leggings of dark cloud, come to us!
With your shirt of dark cloud, come to us!
With your headdress of dark cloud, come to us!

With the zigzag lightning flung over your head, come
    to us, soaring!
With the rainbow hanging high over your head,
    come to us, soaring!
With the zigzag lightning flung out high on the ends
    of your wings, come to us, soaring!
With the rainbow hanging high on the ends of your
    wings, come to us, soaring!

I have made your sacrifice,
I have prepared a smoke for you.

My feet restore for me,
My legs restore for me,
My body restore for me,
My mind restore for me,
My voice restore for me,
Today take out your spell from me.

Far off from me it is taken!
Far off you have done it!
Happily I recover!

Happily my interior becomes cool,
Happily my eyes regain their power,
Happily my head becomes cool,
Happily my legs regain their power,
Happily I hear again!
Happily for me the spell is taken off!

Happily may I walk
In beauty, I walk!

With beauty before me, I walk
With beauty behind me, I walk
With beauty below me, I walk
With beauty above me, I walk
With beauty all around me, I walk

In beauty it is finished.
In beauty it is finished.
In beauty it is finished.
In beauty it is finished.

(From Washington Matthews' *Navajo Legends*.)

Unlike their Athapaskan cousins, the Apache never adapted to alien cultural influences in quite the same way. Whereas the Navajo have shown a capacity to utilize Puebloan, Spanish, Mexican, and Anglo contributions within their own milieu, the Apache have kept more to themselves. A hunting, gathering, and raiding people, they were subdued only with difficulty. It was not until 1886, when Geronimo's Chiricahua band of Apaches finally surrendered, that peace was vouch-

62. Water jar with design of deer and fawns. Height 9·75 in. 1880. Zuni Pueblo, New Mexico. Museum of the American Indian, Heye Foundation, New York

safed in the extreme Southwest.

As a highly nomadic people, the arts and crafts of
55, 56 these people reflect the need for lightweight, unbreak-
able carrying utensils and clothing. They have pro-
50 duced limited quantities of basketry, beadwork, and
leatherwork. Their so-called Devil's Dance mask is used
in coming out ceremonies of young Apache maidens.

The Pueblo Agriculturists

In the Southwest today there are many Puebloan
communities which still maintain a viable economic,
political, and social existence. The Pueblos are classified
by most anthropologists according to major linguistic
groups. The following list shows modern Pueblos as
they are associated by common language:
Keresan-speaking
Western Keresan: Acoma, Laguna
Eastern Keresan: Cochiti, Santo Domingo, San Felipe,
Santa Ana, Zia
Tanoan-speaking
Tiwa: Sandia, Isleta, Picuris (San Lorenzo), Taos
Tewa: San Juan, Santa Clara, San Ildefonso, Nambe,
Tesuque
Towa: Jemez, Pecos (extinct)
Zunian-speaking
Zuni
Shoshonean-speaking Hopi villages
First Mesa: Walpi, Sichomovi, Hano (actually built by
Tewa-speaking Indians from the Rio Grande area

who emigrated after the 1680 Pueblo Revolt),
Polacca
Second Mesa: Shungopovi, Shipaulovi, Mishongnovi,
Toreva
Third Mesa: Hotevilla, Old Oraibi (founded around
1150), New Oraibi, Bacobi

The Tanoan peoples live wholly along the Rio Grande
River in central New Mexico. The Eastern Keresan
people also live in the Rio Grande area but the two
outposts of the Western Keresan are located in western
New Mexico. Zuni Pueblo is situated south of Gallup,
New Mexico, just to the east of the Arizona state line.
The Hopi villages are located on and around their three
mesas in northwest central Arizona, wholly surrounded
by the Navajo.

These people maintain a tradition unbroken since
the days of the Anasazi. While there has undoubtedly
been vast social change and adaptation to various
sorts of conquerors, these people maintain a life that is
organically related to their prehistoric ancestors.

In her classic work on the relationship between
cultural forms and human personality structure, the
late Ruth Benedict had occasion to discuss the Puebloan peoples. In her seminal volume, *Patterns of Culture*,
Benedict describes the contours of Zuni existence in
order to get some perspective on their culture as a
whole. In her work she designates the Zuni as being an
'Apollonian' people. In this brief excerpt from her study,
she makes clear what she means:

*63. Water jar, white slip with deer and geometric design in
brown and black. About 1875. Height 9·5 in. Zuni Pueblo, New
Mexico. Museum of the American Indian, Heye Foundation,
New York*

73

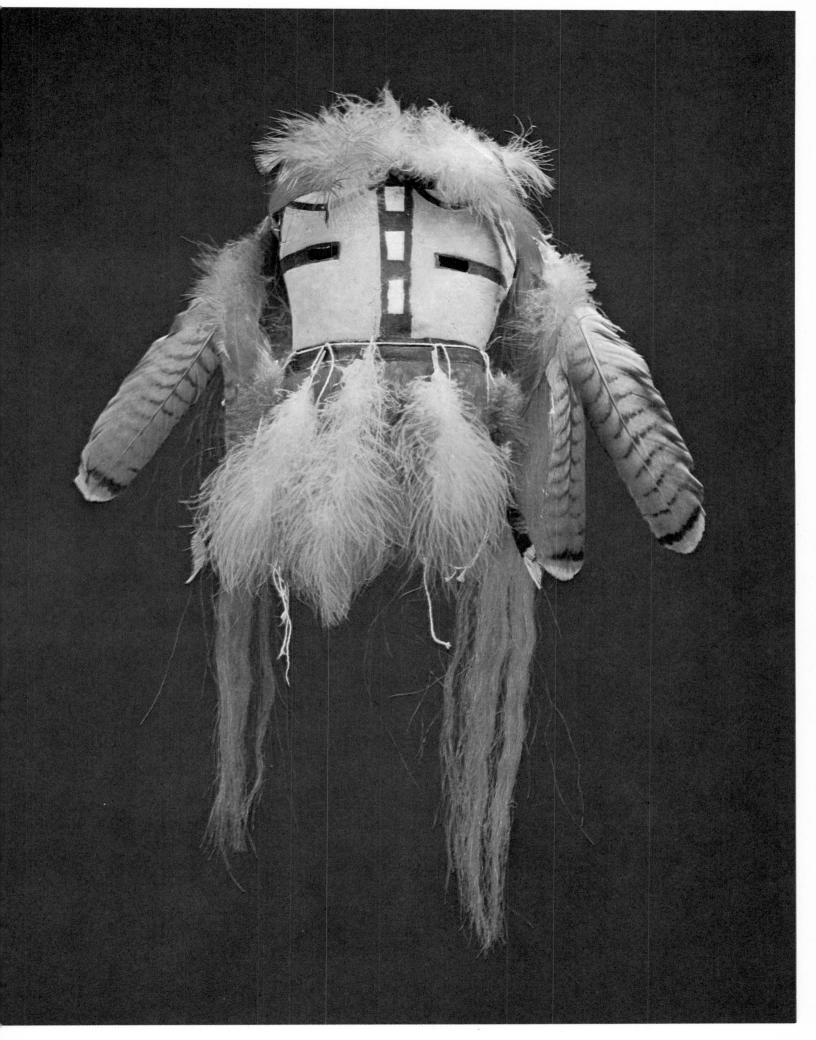

'The basic contrast between the Pueblos and the other cultures of North America is the contrast that is named and described by Nietzsche in his studies of Greek tragedy. He discusses two diametrically opposed ways of arriving at the values of existence. The Dionysian pursues them through "the annihilation of the ordinary bounds and limits of existence"; he seeks to attain in his most valued moments escape from the boundaries imposed upon him by his five senses, to break through into another order to experience. The desire of the Dionysian, in personal experience or in ritual, is to press through it toward a certain psychological state, to achieve excess. The closest analogy to the emotions he seeks is drunkenness, and he values the illuminations of frenzy. With Blake, he believes "the path of excess leads to the palace of wisdom." The Apollonian distrusts all this, and has often little idea of the nature of such experiences. He finds means to outlaw them from his conscious life. He "knows but one law, measure in the Hellenic sense." He keeps the middle of the road, stays within the known map, does not meddle with disruptive psychological states. In Nietzsche's fine phrase, even in the exaltation of the dance he "remains what he is, and retains his civic name."'

Benedict obviously possesses a profound insight into the nature of Pueblo culture. Here indeed are a people for whom the individual *per se* is not the fundamental unit of existence. On the contrary, it is a culture where the group, the whole, the collective are the basic concerns of consciousness. They are a people of 'we,' not 'I.' Even in the conception of fate, the Apollonian Puebloans feel strongly that what happens to one is what happens to all and vice versa. Unlike our Western modes of individualism and liberalism, the Zuni do not look upon society as an instrumental means for the realization of individual ends. The society, in their *Weltanschauung*, is a complete entity and to be an individual is an incomprehensible concept except insofar as he is a part of the whole.

Some of their Apollonian spirit is derived, no doubt, from the very marginal agricultural existence they have (or had in the past). In the precarious kind of living they were able to make for themselves, it was obviously true that the whole people either prospered or suffered together. If one man's crops failed, it was likely that everyone else's did likewise. Success or failure was not a question of individual responsibility and achievement. Survival, in their eyes, was a question of how all the people stood in their relationship with nature and the entirety of cosmic existence. Nature and gods conferred blessings or withheld them to all Puebloan people, not just to one of them. Thus, there is very much a sense of 'all of us together' in their cultural perspective on the world.

This spirit manifested itself in their religious life. These Indians felt strongly that their ceremonials were an integral part, if not cement, of the process which helped to keep together the harmony of the universe. With their ceremonial activities, Katchina cults, and medicine societies, the Puebloans assured the continuance of the eternal cycles of nature and existence itself. How could there be fertility in mother earth, or rain from the skies, or a bountiful harvest, if there were not the positive actions of the people to help maintain these things? And so the people would dance and the *kivas* would be constantly active with religious endeavors. The ceremonial calendar of the Puebloans was very carefully worked out, as were the ceremonials themselves. In accordance with the precepts of a people who did not believe in individualistic undertakings, every detail of costume and each step of a dance was rigorously prescribed and controlled. In this way only could the gods be reassured of the unity of the people and their prayers heard for the continued harmony of the universe.

One of the prices for such a cultural ambience was a pronounced conservatism. Innovation and stylistic changes were difficult to come by for a people so oriented to group norms and values. To be as other-directed as they obviously were is to suggest that deviance of any sort was frowned upon strongly. Social control and strict conformity were hallmarks of these cultures. At no time would an individual wish to stand out from his peers as 'different', for that violated the ethic of 'togetherness' which was cultivated so strongly. The Puebloans possessed several devices, like humor and gossip, in order to control deviance and they exercised these powers whenever needed. Since new ideas and innovations are normally issued from an audacity of imagination, change was very slow and evolutionary since this culture discouraged audacity. Yet, at the same time, such conservativism also generated tenacity and it was that quality which permitted so much of the original culture to endure until the present time. Thus, conservatism of this sort is a double-edged sword: it can thwart cultural innovation but it can also help protect that culture if it is threatened from without.

One of the most attractive characteristics of these people was their commitment to pacifism. The name Hopi, for example, means 'The Peaceful Ones' in their own language. Wars and civil strife, at least in the period before white influence became as predominant as it is, were almost unknown entities for these people. They defended themselves from attack by raiding tribes but never sought out conflict with other peoples.

Concomitant with this quality was the feature of non-competitiveness within the Puebloan community. Unlike our own culture which is so strongly oriented to materialism, power, prestige, and status, the Puebloans denied the necessity for such things. Individuals never compared themselves to others in order to ascertain who might be ahead or behind in some social hierarchy. It was not important for anyone to have more of anything than someone else. Insofar as this was true in their earlier days, the Pueblos had societies which were remarkably egalitarian and democratic. Everyone was of equal importance and worth within the community. If someone was in need, there was someone else who might be able to help out. The search for material wealth, power in office, and prestige in a community were unknown cultural goals.

It is no wonder that many youth of today look to such cultures as the Puebloan for some sort of alternative to the pressures of modern post-industrial society. The example of the Puebloans is esteemed by many of the alienated and anomic within our own milieu. Frank Waters' *The Book of Hopi* became a paperback bestseller as a result of the interest of many in the tenets of such a culture.

The contemporary arts and crafts of these people provide us with renewed assurance that Puebloan culture is still very much alive and viable. Anyone interested in a more in-depth appraisal of these forms should consult Clara Lee Tanner's very excellent *Southwest Indian Craft Arts*. In this volume we will want to survey production in pottery, Katchina dolls, baskets, and silver.

Pottery, as we already know, is an ancient craft surviving to the present time. Since the North American artisan did not possess a potter's wheel, all pottery had to be shaped by hand. In the American Southwest the most common technique is coiling. A pot is built up coil upon coil until it is in the desired shape. Then, the straight-sided coiled pot is shaped from the inside by a gourd shell; and it is also scraped smooth. After the shaping and smoothing process, several slips or coats of fine clay mixed with water are applied. When the pot has dried, it is polished until shiny with a smooth water-worn pebble. The next stage involves the painting of a design on the bowl with a yucca-leaf brush. And finally the vessel is ovenfired at a low temperature. The result, barring any accidents, is a superlative example of the potter's art.

Each Pueblo where the art of pottery is still practised has its own distinctive kind of ceramics. A knowledgeable person can determine where a Pueblo pot might have been made by its type of clay, shape, color and design, and general character. Each village jealously guards its own traditions of pottery and exchanges of design ideas are few. Here are a few of the Pueblos where a notable style of pottery is still made:

Acoma The pottery from Acoma is probably the finest in North America. It can be distinguished by its thin walls and light weight. The best is so thin and hard that it will ring like a bell when struck. Traditional Acoma pottery is polychrome with red and black **59** designs on a white slip depicting flowers, birds, or geometric patterns. Recently, Acoma potters have revived the prehistoric black-on-white designs of Great Pueblo times and the results are outstanding. Some fine artists are Lucy Lewis, Marie Chino, Anita Lowden, and Sarah Garcia.

Zuni Although pottery is rapidly dying out in this Pueblo, due to the fact that most craftswomen are becoming silversmiths, a few owl figurines are still made. In the recent past they made an interesting type of pottery with black-and-red designs on a white slip. Design motifs tended to run towards sunflowers and **62, 63** deer with heart-lines running to their mouths. In terms of texture, Zuni pottery tends to be somewhat brittle. Interesting shalako bowls and fetish jars were also produced in some quantities in the recent past.

Zia As one of the more conservative Pueblos along the Rio Grande, Zia has long prided itself on its pottery heritage. Zia pottery is quite distinctive with designs focusing on the roadrunner (a type of cuckoo), birds, deer, and stylized floral designs. Utilizing a white or tan slip, designs are applied in red or black paint. Zia has long exported its ceramics to other villages who do not make pottery any longer.

Cochiti Cochiti has a tradition of making both bowls and figurines of various sorts. Abstract and floral designs characterize decorations on bowls. Human, bird, and animal figurines have been made in some numbers. Usually the Cochiti employ black paint on a pinkish cream slip for their color scheme.

San Ildefonso Potterymaking at this Pueblo has been of great importance in both historic periods and in the present time. Whereas a form of polychrome pottery was made during the 19th century, 20th-century ceramics at San Ildefonso have tended towards black ware. We cannot discuss pottery at this village without mentioning the name of Maria Martinez. Maria, with her husband Julian, pioneered the production of black ware with matt designs. In the second decade of this century, this couple discovered (or rediscovered) the technique of making black ware. They found out that if smoke from dung is allowed to smother the pot during the firing process, the pot turns black. This polished black ware, often with dull, unpolished designs, has become world famous and has made Maria Martinez a name artist. Maria's two sons, Adam and the late Popovi Da, also came to be noteworthy artists in their own right. Both helped their mother to decorate pottery after the untimely death of Maria's husband, Julian. Popovi Da's distinguished son, Tony Da, has carried on the family tradition in potterymaking. He has launched a series of exciting innovations with regard to the decoration of his pottery, including such things as turquoise and bead inlay on the surface of the pot.

Other notable artists at this village include Rose Gonzales, Blue Corn, Santayana, Desideria Sanchez, and Lupita Martinez. A very excellent polished red **57** ware is also commonly produced at San Ildefonso.

Santa Clara The pottery from this village is remarkably like that of its neighbor, San Ildefonso. Black ware predominates although some artists at Santa Clara also produce a type using white and light red paint on dull red slips. The primary difference between the ceramics of the two Pueblos is that Santa Clara pottery tends to be a bit more massive than that of San Ildefonso. An interesting form of carved black ware is also made by selected artisans at Santa Clara which has proved to be very popular. Some of the fine artists from this village are Teresita Naranjo, the late Serafina Tafoya, Margaret Tafoya, and Christina Naranjo. Very recently several gifted younger potters —including Josef Lonewolf, Grace Medicine Flower, and Margaret and Luther Gutierrez—have initiated new forms of polychrome decoration. The rococo-like flair of some of their surface designs has to be seen to be appreciated.

San Juan Here a distinctive kind of incised pottery is produced which is usually brown in color. A polychrome pottery and highly polished red ware are also made.

Picuris and Taos Pottery from these two Pueblos is very much alike, being plain cooking vessels with mica content in the clay.

Hopi A very distinguished and lovely pottery is made here which has found favor all over the world. Hopi pottery, for the most part, is made only in the First Mesa villages of Hano, Sichomovi, Walpi, and Polacca. Very abstract and highly stylized designs in black, red-orange, or white appear on a cream or orange slip. The artistic sense amongst most of these potters is superior

overleaf 68. Walpi, a Hopi village of the First Mesa.
Photograph by Edward S. Curtis

below 69. Red ware pottery vase made by Alice Cort. Height 11·25 in. Maricopa, Arizona. Museum of the American Indian, Heye Foundation, New York

bottom 70. Male and female dolls in costume with painted body decoration. Height 7 in. Yuma, Arizona. Museum of the American Indian, Heye Foundation, New York

opposite 71. Hemis Katchina doll, carved by Marshal Lomakema, 1972. Height 34 in. Hopi Pueblo, Shongopavi, Arizona. Museum of the American Indian, Heye Foundation, New York

in every way. The most important name associated with Hopi ceramics is clearly Nampeyo. She and she alone was responsible for the Sikyatki revival amongst the women of the First Mesa. Just before the turn of the century, archaeologist Jesse Walter Fewkes was working in the ruins of the Regressive Period Pueblo, Sikyatki. He showed impressive examples of Sikyatki ware to the wife of one of his workmen, Nampeyo, and she reproduced the designs in her own pottery. The striking character of these designs soon captured the imagination of the other women and the Sikyatki revival caught fire. Today the descendants of Nampeyo maintain this distinguished tradition: they include daughters Annie, Fannie and Nellie; granddaughters Daisy Hooee, Rachel, Elva and Leah; and great-grandchildren Priscilla, Dextra Quotskuyva and Lillian. Not only are the designs of Hopi ware appealing but so are the interesting shapes created by these artists. In addition to the Nampeyo family, other noteworthy artists include Garnet Pavatewa, Sadie Adams, Violet Huma, Joy Navasie (*Frog Woman*), and Helen Naha (*Feather Woman*), to name but a few.

Moving from pottery to Katchina dolls, we encounter here an interesting form of woodcarving which is particularly common in the Hopi villages. Katchinas are the spirits that represent animals, plants, flowers, the sun, moon and stars, and legendary figures from Hopi history. Some of them can also be runners, clowns, and escorts to other Katchinas. There are at least 250 of them in Hopi religious life. One legend concerning their origins holds that at one time the Katchina spirits actually lived amongst the Puebloan people in order to help them out. However, being badly treated and even ignored by the Puebloans, they resolved to leave and dwell elsewhere (for the Hopi it is the San Francisco Mountains near Flagstaff, Arizona). Before departing, though, they taught the men how to impersonate them in ceremonial costumes so that the Katchinas would return symbolically to Pueblo villages each year. The Katchina cult is an important one since these deities are considered to be helpful and beneficent to the Puebloan peoples if proper respect is shown.

While the Katchina cult is not confined solely to the Hopi villages—indeed, it is also quite strong at Zuni— it is nonetheless true that it is most commonly manifested amongst this particular group. Two of the manifestations are Katchina dolls and masks which are worn by dancers in ceremonies. The dolls are not considered sacred in themselves but are carved to be given to children in order to instruct them about Katchinas.

Baskets are also produced in many Puebloan villages. The Hopis, in particular, produce two different types of extraordinary quality and beauty. On the Second Mesa coiled basketry is made, and on the Third Mesa wicker baskets are produced. Both kinds are extremely popular with connoisseurs.

And finally, silverwork is an art form which is popular with both the Hopis and Zunis. The Zuni Pueblo produces a great deal of inlay or mosaic jewelry. Preferring several different types of gem stones—turquoise, red coral, black jet, and white mother-of-pearl—these stones are fitted together and glued onto a silver base. The Zunis also make channel-work in which a raised silver grid separates individual stones, and the whole surface is finely polished. The Zunis traditionally have also made pieces of jewelry where many single stones are individually set into bases which are grouped in a cluster.

The Hopis, for their part, are experts with the technique of silver overlay. In its conception it is a simple idea but requires painstaking technical virtuosity on the part of the silversmith. A design is cut out on one sheet of silver and then soldered onto a second sheet of oxidized silver. The resulting effect is very dramatic. The designs are traditional to Hopi culture. With the Hopi, silversmithing is a relatively recent venture, having come into existence in the postwar world as a result of a program at the Museum of Northern Arizona in Flagstaff. It has nevertheless caught on and is now a well-established art form among Hopi craftsmen.

The People of the Desert

The name People of the Desert is given to several tribes living on the western deserts of Arizona: the Pima, Papago, Mojave, Yuma, Maricopa, Chemehuevi, Havasupai, and Walpi. These tribes live in areas where conditions are extremely harsh and opportunities for living are marginal. We believe that the Pima and Papago peoples might be the living descendants of the Hohokam civilization. Other tribes, in prehistoric times, might have served as traders who plied their wares amongst the various cultures of antiquity. Many artisans in these tribes produced both pottery and basketry.

In today's world the Pima and Papago still produce baskets for commercial reasons and they are quite popular.

The Maricopa, Yuma, and Mojave people have one or two women left in each tribe who still make pottery. The Maricopa have traditionally produced a highly polished red ware with black line designs of an abstract nature. The Yuma and Mojave potters made attractive figurines of men and women, perhaps reflecting a dim cultural memory when such Mexican-influenced figurines were common in the prehistoric Southwest.

Modern Painting in the Southwest

A very recent artistic innovation in the American Southwest has been the development of a school of painting. With the increasing acclimatization to Western culture by the Southwestern Indian, it was inevitable, sooner or later, that painting on paper or canvas would be broached.

The artists, writers, and intellectuals of the Santa Fe area began to encourage watercolor painting amongst certain of the Pueblo men in the post World War I period. Such names as John Sloan, Mary Austin, and Alice Corbin Henderson are prominent at this time in the encouragement of several self-taught Pueblo artists. Most of them were from the Pueblo of San Ildefonso (Crescencio Martinez, Julian Martinez, Alfonso Roybal, Awa Tsireh, Abel Sanchez, and Romando Vigil) although Fred Kabotie and Otis Polelonema from Hopi, and Velino (Shije) Herrera (also called Ma Pe Wi) from Zia were also a part of this group. Most of this early painting by self-taught artists was illusionist, representational, and realistic. This is an entirely reason-

72. Watching the dancers. A group of Hopi girls at Walpi.
Photograph by Edward S. Curtis

able state of affairs if we understand that as young men who were acculturated enough to be aware of easel painting, their models would naturally be the narrative and realist art of the white man around them.

Around 1920 to 1925, however, their painting tends to shift from these earlier modes to abstract decoration. The reason for this might be found in the fact that the intellectual community in Santa Fe was interested in seeing that these young men had an Indian style of painting rather than a white man's mode. They must have encouraged these fledgling painters to adhere to traditional Puebloan modes of abstract decoration rather than to European and North American models.

From 1918 to 1925 the Santa Fe Indian School encouraged these young painters, adding some of their weight to such local Santa Fe institutions as the School of American Research and the Museum of New Mexico. All of these forces seem to have had a strong opinion that Indian painting should be different from white art. Insofar as they felt this, they must have pressured these vulnerable young artists to search out other more 'authentic' and 'Indian' approaches to painting. It is not hard to see why many of them reached into traditional Pueblo designs as a viable alternative.

This development in the New Mexico area was

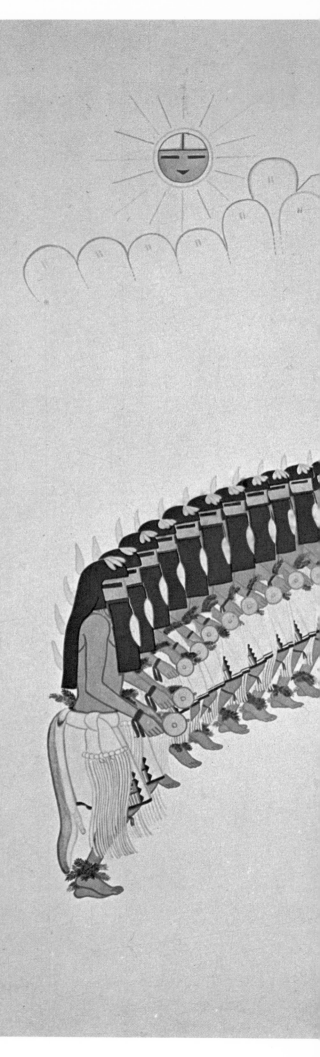

below 73. **Basket Dance** by Oqwa Pi. 14 × 22·5 in. San Ildefonso Pueblo, New Mexico. Museum of the American Indian, Heye Foundation, New York

bottom 74. **Zuni Corn Dance**, by Ray Naha, 1964. Watercolor, 14 × 19 in. Hopi Pueblo, Arizona. Museum of the American Indian, Heye Foundation, New York

opposite 75. **The Delight Makers**, by Fred Kabotie. Watercolor, 20 × 24 in. Hopi Pueblo, Arizona. Museum of the American Indian, Heye Foundation, New York

76. Antelopes and Snakes at Oraibi. The Antelope brotherhood (on the right) and the Snake brotherhood (on the left) take part in the Snake Dance. Photograph by Edward S. Curtis

furthered when Dorothy Dunn came to the Santa Fe Indian School in order to teach art to her young charges. From 1932 to 1937 she devoted herself to the nurturing of young Indian talent in the field of painting. She, like the local intelligentsia before her, was interested in helping Indian painters develop a style which was different from the prevailing white schools. Out of her work during this five-year period came what has come to be known as the 'Santa Fe School.'

In working with her students, Dunn encouraged the development of an especially firm line in drawing and the use of flatly laid colors. The artistic criteria for this work was conditioned by prevailing conceptions of what Indian art should look like, what the Kiowa painters in Oklahoma had worked out in that southern Plains region, and finally, what the recently discovered *kiva* murals of the prehistoric Rio Grande Pueblo of Kuaua suggested in form and content. As a result, Dunn stressed craftsmanlike skills and pictures—for a white market—with a subject-matter of ceremonial, symbolic, ethnographic, or nostalgic content.

Since most of her students were either Puebloan or Navajo, it seemed to make sense to Dunn that these young artists should focus their attention on the traditional life, ceremonials, and designs of their people. From approximately 1915 to 1940, most of the distinguished Indian artists of the Southwest were a product of or influenced by the work of the Indian School at Santa Fe. Some of the distinguished Navajo painters included Harrison Begay, Stanley Mitchell, Gerald Nailor, Quincy Tahoma, and Andy Tsinajinnie. In the Puebloan group there were Jose Rey Toledo, Joe H. Herrera, Ben Quintana, Jose Vicente Aguilar, Pablita Velarde, Vicente Mirabel, and Juan B. Medina.

When we begin to look at the list of more contemporary painters who were a part of the Santa Fe School in one way or another, we are overwhelmed by a multitude of names. It has been a distinguished tradition and one that has gained fame all over the world.

It is not difficult to identify a painting of this school. For the most part, these works show a strong sense of line with flat areas of color, thus giving a strongly two-dimensional effect. The picture itself will likely exhibit a strange combination of mixed realism and abstract symbolism. Very often the central subject-matter will be executed in a more or less realistic manner while the background will be handled in a wholly abstract and symbolic way. There is often no ground line whatsoever or only the hint of one. Subject-matter, as we have said, emphasizes traditional themes and avoids contemporary social comment, on the whole.

While younger artists of native origin are more influenced by contemporary trends in the art world as a whole, they, too, seek to hold onto something that can be termed Indian. At the present Institute for American Indian Arts in Santa Fe, Indian youth from all over the United States has the opportunity to study under distinguished teachers. Here they can learn how to integrate their traditions of the past with contemporary modes of expression. Although the old Santa Fe School style may be coming to an end, as a first kind of paradigm for Indian painters of this region, its contribution has been a lasting and worthy one.

The Plains

In writing about Kiowa painting, Oscar B. Jacobson once said: 'The Anglo-Saxon smashes the culture of any primitive people that gets in his way, and then, with loving care, places the pieces in a museum.' While such a statement is true of North American Indians in general, it bears particular relevance to the plight of the tribes on the Great Plains. Perhaps nowhere else in North America was the aboriginal culture so thoroughly decimated by the greed of the white man. The sharp contrast between the freedom of nomadic life and the despair of sedentary reservation existence is particularly acute for these peoples.

A great deal of romance surrounds the traditional way of life of Great Plains Indians. Everyone is familiar with the stereotype of the feather-bonneted warrior on horseback engaged in the act of buffalo-hunting or warfare. No Indian anywhere has so intrigued the imagination of the world as has the native of the North American Great Plains. The very enumeration of tribal names is sufficient to conjure up a rich association of images: Sioux, Cheyenne, Arapaho, Assiniboine, Blackfeet, Plains Cree, Kiowa, Comanche, Crow, Gros Ventres, and so on.

Many people are not aware, however, that there is also another group of people who were dwellers on the Great Plains. These include such tribes as the Mandan, Hidatsa, Arikara, Caddo, Osage, Kansas, Otos, Omahas, Wichitas, Iowas, Poncas, and Pawnees. These tribal groups are probably the oldest on the Plains. The Great Plains itself is a vast stretch of territory in the heartland of North America: it reaches from the basin of the Saskatchewan River in the north to the central regions of Texas in the south, and from the Mississippi River in the east to the Rocky Mountains in the west. There are actually two sections to the Great Plains; one is the long grass region of the east and the other is the short grass region of the west. In the east there is more rainfall and the soil is more suitable for agriculture, whereas in the west rainfall is quite limited and the soil is much less conducive to raising crops. The latter-named peoples tended to be those who resided in the eastern portions of the American Plains where the rainfall was sufficient for some dependence on agriculture. While less colorful and romantic, perhaps, they are very likely the oldest residents upon the Plains.

The first tribes in this region enjoyed a mode of living that encompassed both agriculture and some hunting and gathering. For the most part, they seemed to rely on their fields where beans, corn, and squash were grown. It appears as if they were able to supplement this diet by engaging in buffalo-hunting forays out on the Plains. Their villages were more or less permanent in nature, being located in fertile areas like the bluffs overlooking river valleys. These tribes, by and large, did not live in conventional tipis but built lodges of more enduring materials. The Mandan in the Missouri River region constructed circular earth-covered abodes that were capable of containing several families, while the more southerly Wichitas, for example, covered their structures with grass matting. On the basis of their agricultural practices and other evidence, we are certain that these peoples had some contact with the Moundbuilders of the American Southeast. Indeed, the life of these more easterly Plains tribes might be interpreted as an extension of the eastern Woodlands culture that goes back to prehistoric times; modified, of course, by the conditions and circumstances of the Plains.

These peoples, as we have said, were amongst the earliest to hunt the buffalo. Doing so before the advent of the horse, they devised approaches to buffalo-hunting that were most ingenious. One method was to lure a buffalo herd close to the edge of a high bluff or cliff in order to drive them over *en masse*. One hunter might masquerade as a buffalo bull and attract the attention of the leaders of the herd by his mimicry. He would then gradually lead the herd closer and closer to the precipice where other members of the hunting party would lie in wait behind natural or artificial camouflage. At a given signal, the buffalo impersonator would leap out of danger and the herd would be stampeded over the drop-off with wild cries and whoops by the others. Down below, more hunters would be positioned to finish off any buffalo not killed by the fall and women would begin the immediate butchering of the animals. Another method would be to construct a 'buffalo pound' or enclosure where the beasts could be trapped and slaughtered. Since the horse was virtually non-existent on the Plains until around 1700 or later, these are the most time-honored techniques of hunting.

Many of the tribes we are most apt to associate as archetypal of the classic Plains culture were actually late-comers to the region. The coming of the white man was fundamental to many historic developments with regard to Indian culture, and nowhere is that more readily seen than in the case of the Plains. From approximately 1650 to 1850, North America was the arena of white exploitation for the fur trade. Particularly in the eastern forest regions, the Canadian Shield, and the northern Plains, the white man exhibited an insatiable appetite for furs and pelts of all sorts. In this whole region, many Indian tribes were marshalled into the service of rich fur companies for the purpose of

77. Bear Bull, Blackfoot.
Photograph by Edward S. Curtis

78. Man's vest with geometrical beaded design. Oglala Sioux.
Museum of the American Indian, Heye Foundation,
New York

either trapping or serving as middlemen. The economic significance of this activity to the European colonial nations was immense. As Europeans sought to use the New World as a hinterland for their rapidly industrializing economies, aboriginal ways of life in North America underwent transformation owing to these alien forces. This transformation explains, in large part, the populating of the Plains by whole new tribes during this period.

The Cree and Ojibway tribes became the prosperous middlemen of the big fur-trading companies in the region around the Great Lakes and north into the Canadian Shield. They were the first to receive guns and ammunition in this area and they were pre-eminent as powerful go-betweens. They would take furs from the tribes who actually did much of the trapping, like the Chipewyans of the Far North, and present them to the white man for the final sale. Such a middleman operation was quite profitable for the Cree and Ojibway, and they quite naturally wanted to control as large an area as possible in order to derive such gains. Thus, the Cree and Ojibway began a process of territorial expansion and subjugation of neighboring tribes that was to become of central importance in the development of the Plains.

In their expansion, these two Algonkian-speaking tribes enjoyed a considerable advantage. They possessed weaponry which was invariably far in advance of those Indians who were more removed from the arena of trading operations with the white man. Not only did they possess riches in trading goods that were well nigh irresistible to many poorer tribes, but they also had the power in military terms to enforce their will on those who would not cooperate. What this meant was that the Cree and Ojibway sought to drive from their lands those people who would not place themselves in a position to be useful to the new trading hierarchy.

Many of the tribes who later came to be singularly identified as classic Plains people—like the Sioux, Cheyenne, and Arapaho—were originally Woodlands dwellers. Pressurized by the better armed Ojibway (who were most dominant in the Great Lakes area), bands of these tribes gradually found their way onto the Plains. They adapted, of course, to the new ecological demands of their environment. In such a manner and in historic times did the Plains become the home of new peoples.

Even the Cree and Ojibway themselves succumbed to the lure of the Plains in their process of expansion. Knowing that there were rich sources of meat, particularly useful in dried form as pemmican for fur traders in the wilderness, these two tribes had many bands which wandered out into the Plains and gradually came to settle there. Portions of these tribes ultimately decided to live permanently upon the Plains, and as such they adopted new customs and embraced classic cultural Plains styles. They became so different from their Woodlands cousins that they had to be known by new names: the Plains Cree and Plains Ojibway (or Bungi).

Therefore, in a period beginning after 1700 or so, the Great Plains became host to a new series of people who had to adopt new modes of living in response to a new environment.

The Sioux are an interesting illustration of what we have just been discussing. The Sioux (sometimes called Dakota) were originally an eastern-dwelling Woodlands tribe that might have had its earliest sources in the American Southeast. Living in Minnesota before the 1700 period, they came under heavy pressure from enemy Ojibway bands who were exceedingly ambitious and far better armed. In fact, the name 'Sioux' is actually a French Canadian abbreviation of the original Ojibway term for them which was Nadowessioux (or Nadowessi) which means 'small snake' or 'enemy.'

The Ojibway engaged in a series of wars with the Sioux, and as a result many bands of the latter tribe were forced westward. While a few Sioux people did remain in the Minnesota area, most of them were strung out westwards from that original point. Ultimately, the Sioux divided themselves into three generic groups according to geographic locale. In the east there were the Santee Sioux, in the western Minnesota region from the Mississippi River to the Red River. The major Santee bands were the Mdewakantan, Sisseton, Wahpekute, and Wahpeton. In the center there were the Yankton and Yanktonai Sioux occupying the area between the Red River and the Missouri River in North and South Dakota. Finally, in the west, there were the Teton Sioux who wandered the region from the Missouri River as far west as the Yellowstone and Big Horn Rivers. The important bands of the Teton branch were the Hunkpapa, Oglala, Brulé, Minneconjou, Sans Arc, Two Kettles, and Sihasapa.

It was the western Teton Sioux who were most prominent in the wars against white encroachment during the 1860s and 1870s. Out of the doomed struggle of these people to protect and perpetuate their way of life came such Teton heroes as Red Cloud, Sitting Bull, Rain-in-the-Face, Crazy Horse, Gall, Crow King, Young-Man-Afraid-of-his-Horses, and so many others.

The two keys to understanding the classic Plains life as we have come to know it from 1700 on are the buffalo and the horse. In actual fact, the classic period was a relatively short-lived one in Indian history: it did not begin until 1700 at the very earliest and by the 1860s it was already coming to a close as a result of the white man's encroachment. After a brief span of only 150 years, white demands that the Plains Indians give up his nomadic existence and settle upon reservations caused the destruction of that culture. In the 1860s and 1870s the white man enforced his demands by encouraging the effective extinction of buffalo herds and by applying vicious military pressure.

The buffalo was in point of fact the prime variable in the Plains way of life. Without the buffalo there would have been no classic culture. The buffalo provided for almost every tangible need of these people and was the factor which made their nomadic life both a necessity and a possibility. His flesh provided the Plainsman with food, his hide provided him with clothing and tipi covering, his bones became utensils, his sinew was used as thread, his brains were the stuff out of which paste was made, and even his droppings were 'buffalo chips' that made excellent fuel for fires. The buffalo, quite literally, was a walking department store for Indian needs, and as their economy was built upon his existence, so was the remainder of their culture.

The horse was the second major foundation for Plains Indian life. Insofar as these later tribes did not have agriculture as a fundamental guarantor of livelihood, they had to depend on being near to the buffalo for continued sustenance. Since the buffalo was a migratory animal, they too had to wander, at least to some measure. The horse made that nomadic existence a real possibility. With the horse these people could move about as they never had before.

The Spanish introduced the horse into the American Southwest during the 1600s. Although they were careful not to let these animals fall into the hands of neighboring Indians, the Pueblo Revolt of 1680 resulted in large herds of these horses being loosed upon the land. Indians of this southern region soon learned how to utilize and domesticate the horse. From these origins, the use of the horse spread in an easterly and northerly direction. By the 1740s most Indians of the central and southern Plains were mounted, and by 1770 even the most northerly Plains Cree and Assiniboine were in possession of them.

It was the horse which unleashed many of the potentials in Plains Indian life. While he was not so fundamental in importance as the buffalo, the horse made

life a lot easier and more interesting. While buffalo were still hunted in the old ways with drives and pounds, they could also be sought out on horseback. Moving from camp to camp, facilitated by the presence of the horse, greater distances could be travelled and more goods hauled by horse travois than was possible before. **105**

The horse also contributed to new developments in warfare and the amassing of wealth. While the Plains Indian had an ongoing tradition of war before the advent of the horse, with this new means of mobility whole new possibilities opened up before the Plains warrior. Now armed bands of adventurers could travel over many miles in order to make contact with a far away enemy. Because of increased mobility and the importance of the control of hunting grounds, warfare became more pronounced everywhere. The Plains Cree and Assiniboine, for example, joined together in an alliance in order to exterminate Blackfeet, Sioux, and Gros Ventres influence from the region of the Saskatchewan River system. The control of these hunting grounds was vital for the economic viability of these tribes, both in terms of their self-contained economy and the possibilities of the area with regard to the fur trade. Thus, with the horse and the new

weapons of the white man, great areas became the subject of contention.

Despite the fact that contention over land was an important reason for warfare, it was not the only cause. War was also a means whereby a warrior could gain honor, prestige, and status within his tribal community. No young man could be counted as having arrived at manhood without validating his claim by going on a raiding party. Groups of ambitious and anxious warriors might gather together and pledge themselves to engage in hostilities with some enemy. In these kinds of encounters, the object was never to annihilate a whole people. On the contrary, the object was to secure honor and prestige by certain stylized successes.

One of the key disadvantages of the Plains Indian in his protracted conflict with the white man was that he did not understand war in the way that his enemy practised it. For whites the aim of conflict with the Indian was clear: eliminate the freedom of Indian people upon the Plains either by exterminating them

in toto or by forcing them to acquiesce to existence on concentration camp-like reservations. The Indian did not comprehend this. While many of the more astute and experienced chiefs did, the Indian masses as a whole did not really understand what it was the white man intended until it was too late. When the United States went to war it intended to conquer whole areas of real estate and eliminate the capacity of an entire people to carry on with their former existence. The Indian simply did not wage war for that kind of purpose. For him, war was a means to gain individual notoriety and fame; to exterminate a people, even though they be his enemy, was not within his goal system. Thus, he was not prepared for the war of annihilation which the white man waged.

For a Plains Indian, battle was an opportunity to gain a point (or count coup) over an enemy. Often it would be less desirable to kill an enemy (even though one might be able to) than to simply touch him and let him go on living. More honor could be gained by striking a living enemy warrior than by perfunctorily killing an

96

82. Woman's dress with beaded decoration. Yankton
Sioux, South Dakota. Museum of the American Indian,
Heye Foundation, New York

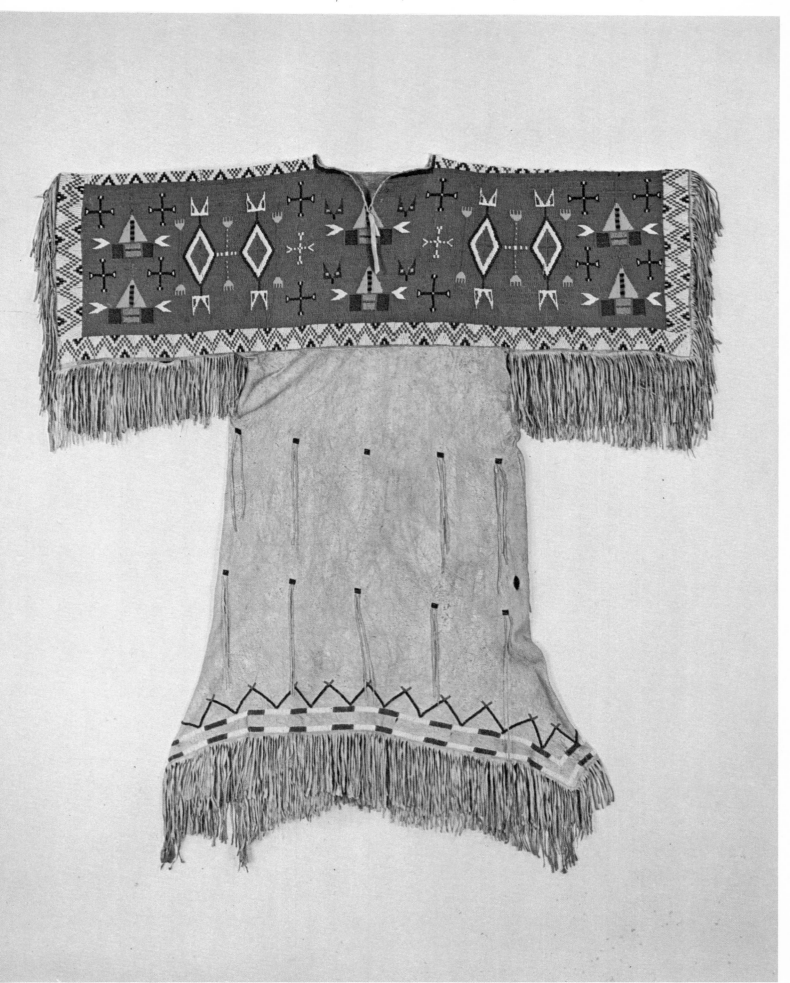

below 83. Woman's dress with beaded decoration, worn
only by a woman who has given a Sun Dance. Piegan,
Piegan Reservation, southern Alberta, Canada. Museum of
the American Indian, Heye Foundation, New York

opposite above 84. Painted elkskin robe with scene of a
buffalo hunt. Width about 50 in. Crow, Montana. Museum of
the American Indian, Heye Foundation, New York

opposite below 85. Painted parfleche bag. Width 17 in.
Sioux, South Dakota. Museum of the American Indian,
Heye Foundation, New York

86. Mandan Bull Society Dance, *by Carl Bodmer. A frenzied ceremony held periodically to draw the elusive buffalo herds closer to the villages. British Museum, London*

below 87. Tipi lining, quilled and painted decoration showing Indians on horseback. 68 × 86 in. Teton Sioux. Museum of the American Indian, Heye Foundation, New York

opposite 88. Beaded deerskin with box-and-border design. Oglala Dakota, South Dakota. Museum of the American Indian, Heye Foundation, New York

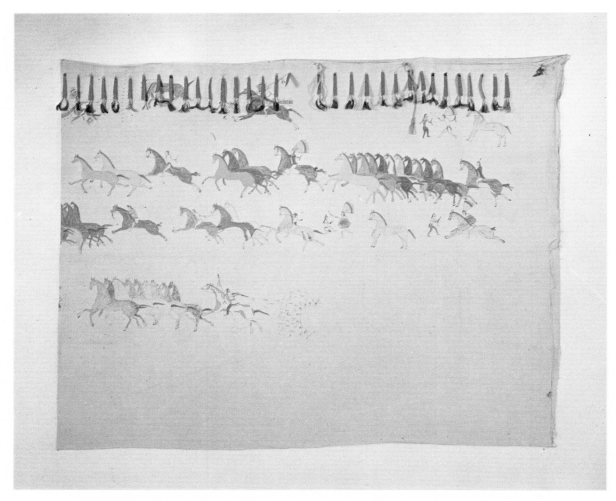

individual one had already vanquished. It might be far more prestigious to sneak into an enemy camp and steal horses from out under the noses of the owners than to sweep down upon a sleeping people simply for the purpose of killing. Moreover, as the horse became more and more a symbol of wealth and well-being for the Plains Indian, horse-stealing expeditions emerged as a popular form of raiding. A man with many horses was a wealthy man indeed. Towards the end of the 19th century, horse-stealing was both a popular and profitable pastime for upward mobile young warriors. In such a way, then, warfare was a means for accumulating honors and wealth rather than a concerted effort to end existence for a group of people.

The individualism of Indian violence had little in common with the mass atrocities of the white man. Given the fact that the white man also had superior weaponry, there was hardly any contest. All the Indian had was his courage, cunning, and knowledge of the terrain. While this could stand him in good stead for a while, in the long run it was not enough. To fight with an enemy dedicated to the ending of your existence—given also his superiority in both numbers and weapons—and not to face him with similar intentions is to define the nature of an unequal contest.

The will of the Plains Indian was also severely weakened by his experience with white man's diseases and alcohol. The Indian did not possess natural immunity to many diseases—like measles, smallpox, tuberculosis, venereal disease, etc.—unlike his European counterpart, and so was prey to their ravages. Wave after wave of epidemics hit Indian villages in the 1830s, 1840s, and 1850s, with the inevitable result of a high death rate. The Mandans were virtually wiped out in a smallpox epidemic in the 1840s, and the Assiniboines lost over half their population to one in the 1830s. As if this was not bad enough, unscrupulous fur traders seduced inexperienced Indians with vast quantities of rotgut alcohol. Being vulnerable to its effects, many an Indian trapper would recklessly barter away a whole year's work in order to have a three-day drunk as his only reward. The effects of alcohol were devastating. Whole bands might be incapacitated for periods of time, unable to engage in hunting or gathering to provide for their needs. The cheating and deceit implicit in the policies of many fur-trading firms, as manifested in the sale of liquor to Indian trappers, is a dark blot on the record of Indian-white relations. The double scourge of disease and alcohol is still with the Indian.

Nevertheless, in the days of freedom, life on the Great Plains had much to recommend it. In the summer the tribe would gather together again in order to commence the buffalo-hunting season with a great Sun Dance. Here there would be a renewal of kinship

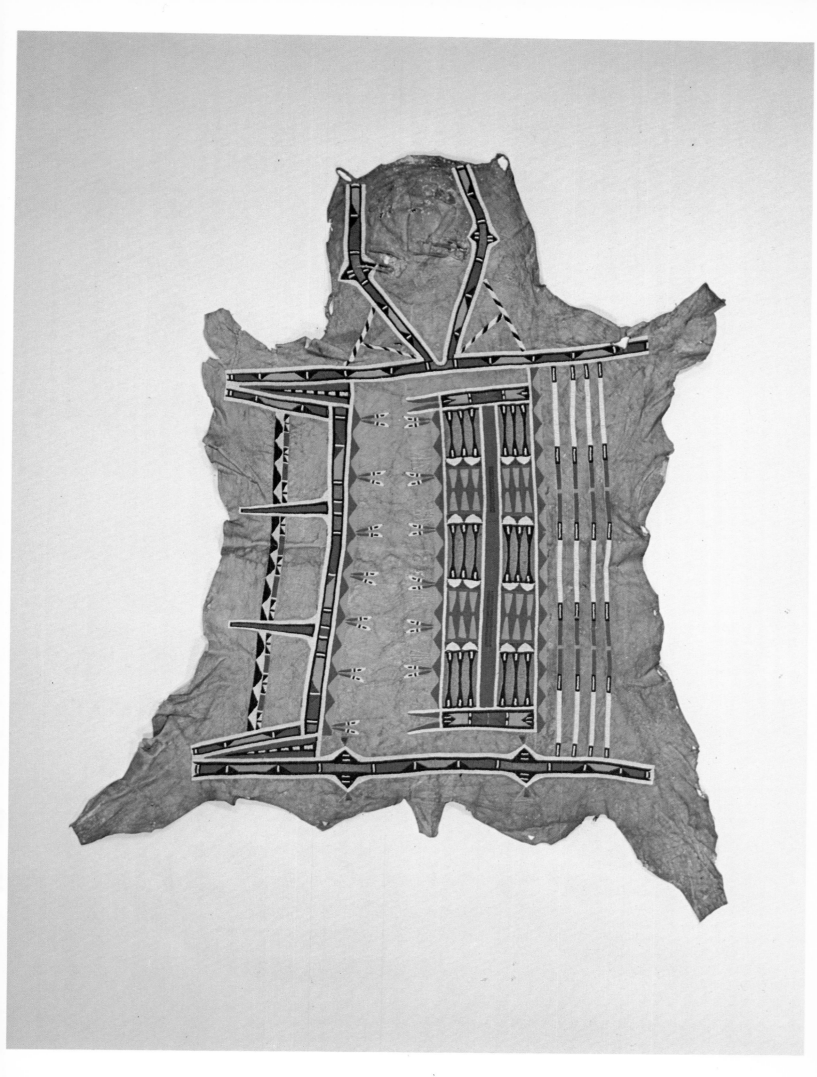

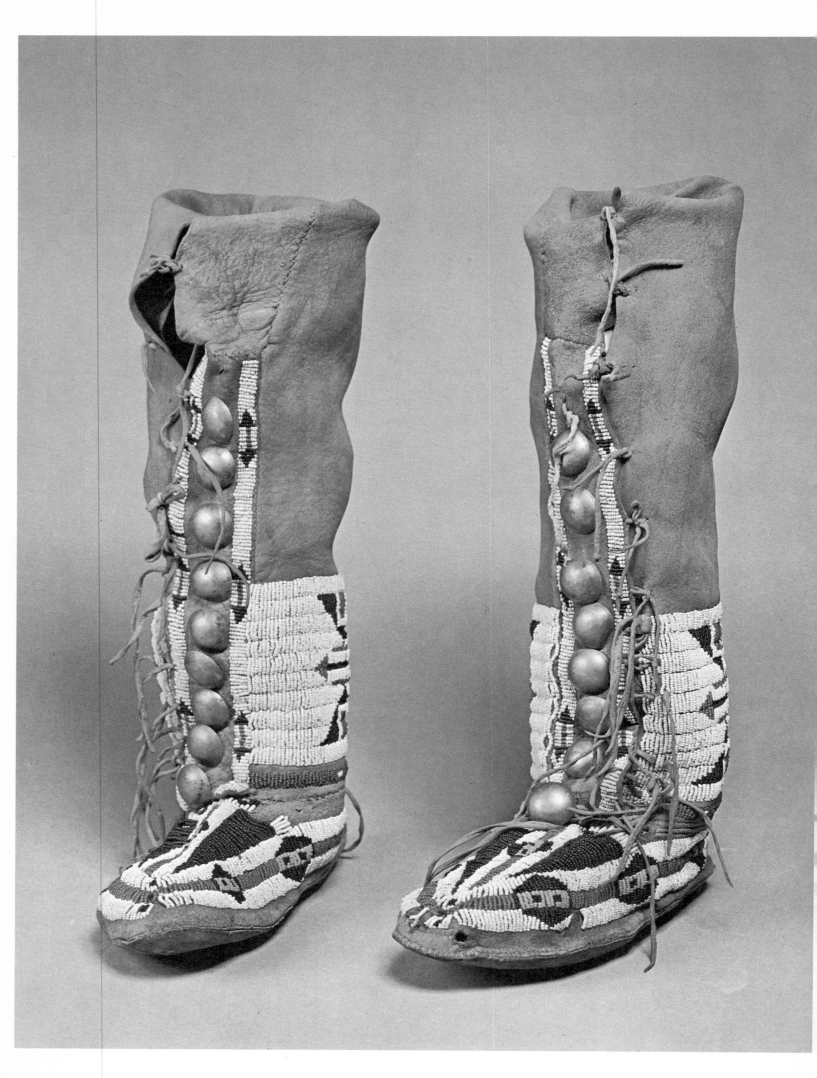

opposite 89. Pair of legging moccasins with beaded decoration. Cheyenne, Wyoming. Museum of the American Indian, Heye Foundation, New York

below 90. Headdress made of ermine skin and buffalo horns. Length 28 in. Piegan, Piegan Reservation, southern Alberta, Canada. Museum of the American Indian, Heye Foundation, New York

bottom 91. Beaded baby carrier. Length 43 in. Kiowa, Oklahoma. Museum of the American Indian, Heye Foundation, New York

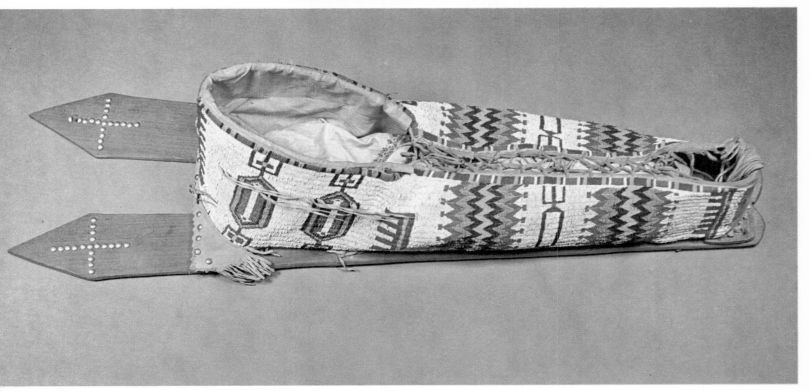

and political ties when the tribe could call itself one again. Courting and sports activity would be attendant to such a conclave. The central purpose of these meetings, most obviously, was a religious observance.

Amongst tribes like the Sioux or Blackfeet, one or more young men might offer to undergo ordeals of sacrifice and torture in the Sun Dance. It was considered especially significant if a young warrior were to indicate that he would represent the people in an ordeal of painful dimensions. In such a ceremony he would have muscles in his chest, legs, and arms pierced with bone skewers. Thongs would be attached to these bones which were connected, in turn, to the lodge poles of the roof of the Sun Dance structure. The warrior would then spin or gyrate and otherwise seek to tear the bone skewers from his flesh. The excruciating pain of this ordeal, made even worse by thirst, might go on for quite some while before the skewers were torn loose or the man would faint with

exhaustion. Although he would carry the scars of such an experience with him for life they would be marks of honor, and the young man would be venerated by all for what he had done for them. Sitting Bull is reputed to have had a vision foretelling the events of the Battle of the Little Big Horn (when General George Armstrong Custer and his 7th Cavalry were wiped out) during the course of a Sun Dance in 1876.

81

Not all Plains Indians, however, had such physical ordeals connected with their Sun Dance. The Plains Cree and Assiniboine, for example, possessed no torture ritual with their version of this ceremony. For all tribes it was a time of prayer, contemplation, spiritual renewal, and a mystical search for the essence of the universe.

In the spiritual realm, as well, we find the Spirit Quest of the young man around the time of puberty. When a boy was ready to become a man he was prepared by his father and a shaman for the experience of a vision

above 94. *Pair of quilled moccasins. Cheyenne, Wyoming. Museum of the American Indian, Heye Foundation, New York*

below 95. *Gun case with beaded decoration. Length 41 in. Assiniboine, Canada. Museum of the American Indian, Heye Foundation, New York*

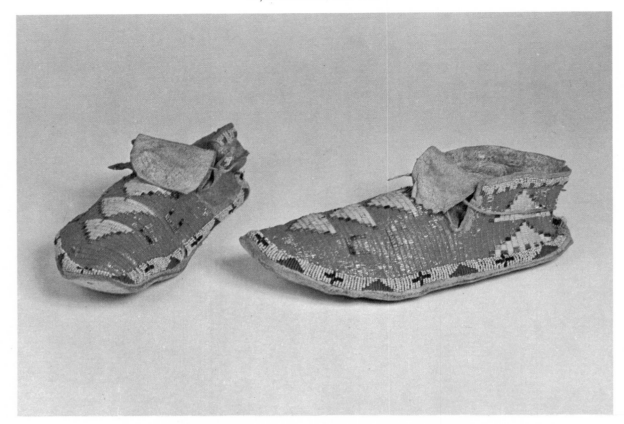

below 97. Buffalo hide shield decorated with paint, feathers
and a dried bird's head. Diameter 24 in. Crow, Montana.
Museum of the American Indian, Heye Foundation, New York

quest. It was intended that the boy leave his village and go out into the wilderness in order to fast, think, and wait for a mystical experience. If all went properly, the boy would have a vision and in that vision he would see and know the truth which his life would have for him. Very likely he would envisage some animal that might be a symbol for him in suggesting what his life as a man would be like. Upon his return from the vision quest, the boy was ready to be considered a man.

The arts and crafts of such a people clearly reflect a mode of life where the buffalo and horse were key facts of existence. Objects produced by these nomadic people had to be both utilitarian and portable. Since moving was a frequent phenomenon, everything made had to be relatively compact and easily transportable. These requirements resulted in a concentration on hide articles. The hide of the buffalo was the basis of 97 clothing, tipi covers, shields, baby carriers, medicine bundles, and so on. The decoration of these items constituted the primary contribution of the Plains Indian to arts and crafts. Painting and quillwork or beadwork embroidery were the two most important forms of decoration.

Painted decoration is found on a variety of hide objects. Natural pigments were used to decorate such 85 things as parfleches (flat rawhide containers), shields, robes, tipi covers, and some articles of clothing. Painting tended to be of two distinct sorts: geometric and naturalistic.

It is probable that the earliest sort of decoration was executed utilizing basic geometric motifs. These motifs, of course, invariably have a symbolic meaning. The designs also tended to become stylized over a period of time. These generic geometric motifs were of two sorts: solar and celestial designs on the one hand and earth symbols (or what Norman Feder in *American* 88 *Indian Art* has termed 'box-and-border design') on the other. The first type consisted of an arrangement of several concentric circles. The second type witnessed complicated strips of angular arrangements. These designs are usually found on robes; the men wore the solar and celestial variety while the women wore those with earth motifs.

Later on, we believe, naturalistic decoration also came into vogue among the men. Most painting of this nature involves the narration of some personal experience of war, hunting, or horse-stealing. It has been termed naturalistic because there is some attempt to portray men, horses, and buffalo realistically. It was considered wholly legitimate for a man to boast of his exploits and achievements in such a manner; provided 84 only that he tell the truth. Therefore, on robes, tipi 87 covers or shields, a man would paint the history of his real-life experiences. While the human figures are often drawn in a stiff and stick-like fashion, horses and bison tend to be more fully sketched.

Where the notion for such naturalistic work came from is problematical. Anthropologist and historian John C. Ewers believes that some of the impetus for such an art form could have come from contact with white artists and illustrators. European art during the 18th and 19th centuries was both representational and naturalistic, and Indians would have had a reasonable number of opportunities to study this style through reproductions in books, magazines, and so on. Even

more importantly, white artists like George Catlin and Carl Bodmer journeyed throughout the northern Plains region in the 1830s in order to paint the landscape and its native inhabitants. They report how fascinated many of the Indians were with their work and how anxious some of them were to learn more. It is not impossible that the much-heralded visits of these early artists had something to do with the development of naturalistic art among the Plains Indians.

Be that as it may, naturalistic painting of male exploits was very common in the period from 1850 to 1880. This sort of art was carried one step further when certain captured warriors were given paper and drawing materials in order to while away their time during their incarceration at various forts. They were encouraged to draw scenes from their life like those they put on hides. It was an easy step for many of them to go from hides to paper and the results are fascinating. One Cheyenne warrior imprisoned at Fort Marion, Florida, in 1875, named Cohoe (or Lame Man), made several sketches which have become quite famous. They show what his life must have been like in the 'old days.' Sometimes these sketches were made as an act of remembrance during reservation days, as was the case with Amos Bad Heart Bull. Bull painted a number of pictures between 1890 and his death in 1913 on the Pine Ridge Indian Reservation. This Oglala Sioux produced more than 400 drawings during this period. The publication of his work in 1967 was a major event in the history of North American Indian arts. In any case, the connection between the work of such men as Cohoe and Amos Bad Heart Bull and their predecessors is direct. As an artistic style, it portrays a strong white influence even at its inception.

In more recent times, after the unfortunate period of 1890 to the 1920s that was especially pronounced in Plains Indian art, a new school of painting has developed on the southern Plains of the United States. It is called the 'Oklahoma School' since most of the events surrounding the development of this style took place in that state. In the period 1917 to 1926, an Indian Service field matron named Susan Peters organized an arts club for some young Kiowa boys near Anadarko, Oklahoma. Around 1926 or 1928 the Kiowas under Susan Peters' tutelage were enrolled in special courses at the University of Oklahoma. Here the youths came in contact with Edith Mahier and Oscar B. Jacobson in the Art Department. The five Kiowa men involved in this project—Spencer Asah, James Auchiah, Jack Hokeah, Stephen Mopope, and Monroe Tsa Toke— 108 were the founding fathers of the Oklahoma School.

Jacobson, an exponent of the American art moderne style of 1920 to 1940, heavily influenced their development as a group and as individuals. He worked with them in order to evolve a style of painting that had 106 strong links with traditional forms yet had a modern 107 approach. What emerged from their efforts was a style that emphasizes, according to J. J. Brody (in *Indian Painters And White Patrons*), flat colours, clear outlines, sinuous curves, and an emphasis on line which is used to separate discrete color areas. The subject-matter is primarily nostalgic in that it harks back to traditional themes of dancing, warfare, buffalo-hunting, horses, and so on. It might be said, in general, that the work of the Oklahoma School tends to be more design-

100. Atsina (Gros Ventres) warriors.
Photograph by Edward S. Curtis

below left 101. Breast ornament for a horse with beaded decoration. Length 42 in. Crow, Montana. Museum of the American Indian, Heye Foundation, New York

bottom 103. Buckskin Ghost Dance shirt with painted design of birds and stars. Arapaho. Museum of the American Indian, Heye Foundation, New York

below right 102. Pipe bag with beaded and quilled decoration representing an Indian in costume and an Indian riding a horse. Length 39 in. Blackfoot, Montana. Museum of the American Indian, Heye Foundation, New York

opposite 104. Beaded baby carrier with floral design. Length 37.5 in. Kutenai, Montana. Museum of the American Indian, Heye Foundation, New York

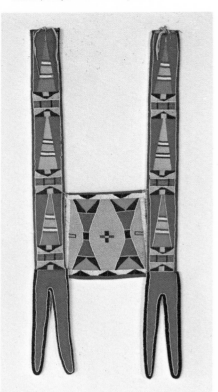

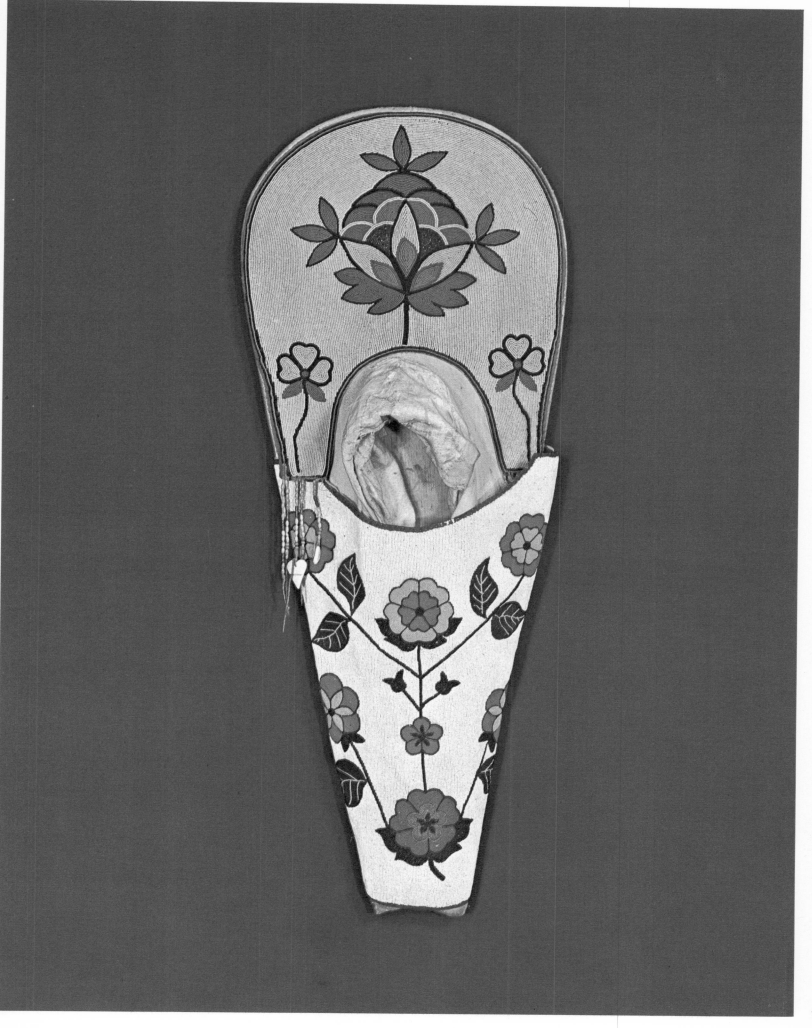

105. A Blackfoot travois. The travois was the most common means of transporting possessions amongst the Indians living on the Plains. In the days before the horse a smaller version of the travois was drawn by dogs. Photograph by Edward S. Curtis

oriented—even to the degree that some of the paintings are more emblems than stories—than content-
oriented. It goes without saying that the work done by
these Kiowa artists also influenced developments at
the Santa Fe Indian School where Dorothy Dunn
taught in the 1930s.

The painting executed on the northern Plains is
quite different from that of the southern Plains Oklahoma School. In the states of Wyoming, Montana,
Idaho, and the Dakotas, as well as in the Canadian
provinces of Alberta, Saskatchewan, and Manitoba,
artists were largely untouched by the developments in
Oklahoma. Here the painters continued a tradition of
realism begun in the 19th century. Whereas the Kiowa
and Comanche were strongly influenced by white
tutors in the development of a hybrid style, the northern Sioux, Assiniboine, Gros Ventres, Flathead, Blackfeet, and Plains Cree painters of this region were
largely left to follow their own means of expression.

The primary characteristic of these mainly self-
taught painters is that of realism. This style is the product, in part, of an exposure to the popular art of the
white man's world. Ever since the fateful trips of such
white artists as George Catlin, Carl Bodmer, and Paul
Kane to the Plains area in the 1830s and 1840s, the
painting of northern Plains artists has tended to become
ever more naturalistic. With the advent of reservation
life and the partial deculturation of once nomadic
tribes, their arts—as with other elements of their culture
—have experienced the effect of cultural contact with
the surrounding white milieu. The omnipresent examples of the white man's creativity—particularly with

respect to European realism and romanticism—were
not without effect on the imagination of northern
Plains Indian painters. However, these artists have
take this kind of realistic perspective and the concept
of art for art's sake and wedded it to a unique imagination of their own. The unique form of art which results
from this fusion is one with whole new dimensions of
meaning and beauty.

One example of this work is found in the painting of
the Oglala Sioux, Roscoe White Eagle from the Fort
Peck Indian Reservation in Montana. His distinguished
ancestor was White Eagle who was with Sitting Bull at
the Battle of the Little Big Horn against Colonel Custer
in 1876. His grandson utilizes striking colours in his
canvases which deal, in the main, with Sioux history
and tribal life as it used to be in the old days.

Another example of northern Plains painting comes
from a Plains Cree artist of Saskatchewan named Allen
Sapp. Sapp specializes in interpreting scenes from
Indian life when he was a boy growing up on the Red
Pheasant Reserve in the 1930s and 1940s. In his work he
goes beyond realism to provide the viewer with a mood
and feeling for the life of his people as it used to be a
generation ago. Sapp is particularly skilled in evoking
a sense of winter in the Saskatchewan parklands with
its unbelievable cold, dry snow, and frozen bush.

To move on to the subject of quillwork and beadwork decoration, it is immediately apparent that
Plains art reached a very high degree of excellence in
this field. Before the coming of the white man only
porcupine quills were used since beads were non-
existent (except for rare shell imports from the Pacific

coast). Beads were first introduced by fur traders in the eastern Woodlands around 1675. Large 'pony' beads did not reach the Plains until around 1800. The small 'seed' beads that are so common today were not introduced until around 1840 and did not become popular till 1860 or so. Thus, the geometric embroidered decoration that we admire so much today was executed primarily in quillwork during most of the classic Plains period.

When beadwork did become common, two types of sewing became most general. For some tribes the lazy-stitch was predominant while for others the spot-stitch was most characteristic.

Amongst the Sioux, Cheyenne, and Arapaho, the lazy-stitch technique was most frequently used. With this method short rows of beads are laid down parallel to each other and fastened to the material only at the ends, the final result being rows of parallel ridges. This type of beadwork has much the same appearance as the earlier quillwork. This technique, by its very nature, **78, 82** demands a geometric design, as does quillwork. Sioux, Cheyenne, and Arapaho designs are similar in that they are based upon simple modular geometric blocks which are then elaborated with filigree-like ornamentation. They can be contrasted with the geometric **95** designs of the more northerly tribes such as the Assini- **80, 92** boine, Blackfeet, or Plains Cree. Here the modular geometric blocks stand alone without ornamentation except, perhaps, for an outline in a contrasting colour to the background; the shades used were usually simple primary colours.

Amongst the tribes of the northern Plains and Plateau area, spot-stitching became a popular technique. This was done by laying threaded beads on the material and then sewing each bead in place. This type of beading is much more flexible in that it allows for considerable variation in design. Many of the tribes of the northern Plains maintained their preference for geometric motifs only in the early stages of the introduction of this technique. Then, seeing the possibilities implicit within this technique, they began to experiment with floral designs originating in the Woodlands (see page 155). This development was true not only with the Plains Cree and Assiniboine but occurred amongst the Blackfeet and Crow as well. Moreover, floral designs were very popular in the Plateau region with such **104** tribes as the Nez Percé, Kutenai, Bannock, and Cayuse. In the extreme northwest portion of the Plateau region, amongst tribes like the Umatilla, very realistic bead- **99** work of zoomorphic and anthropomorphic forms became popular. The flexibility inherent in the spot-stitching method permitted a great many distinctive developments in the medium.

With the ending of the classic period of Plains life and the beginning of the reservation period, many of the fine old arts and crafts went into a precipitous decline. The despair of these people is difficult to imagine. They had no choice, however. Either they had to accept the meaninglessness of reservation existence or be exterminated. With the disappearance of the buffalo herds as a result of excessive hunting in the 1870s and early 1880s, the Plains Indian had no alternative but to accept the inevitable. To resist further would have meant that they were to become 'good Indians,' in the sense that 'the only good Indian is a dead Indian.' (Dee Brown, in *Bury My Heart at Wounded*

Knee, points out that in 1868 a Comanche named Tosawi brought in his band to Fort Cobb in the Valley of Washita to surrender to General Philip Sheridan. In speaking to the General in broken English, the Indian said, 'Tosawi, good Indian.' Sheridan then replied, 'The only good Indians I ever saw were dead.' In time his words, in simplified form, became a famous American aphorism.)

As with any despairing people who have lost control over their own destiny, they were vulnerable to Messianic religions. In the late 1880s one came out of Nevada. A medicine man by the name of Wovoka dreamed that he had entered the presence of the Great Spirit and this Holy One had assured him that He had not forgotten His red children. He grieved at how the white man had treated His only begotten Son on earth and had resolved to save the Indian from the yoke of the white man in North America. One day, he promised, a great cloud would cover the earth and on it would be all the buffalo and Indian people who had disappeared as a result of white oppression. This cloud would bury the white man and all his works as it returned these beings to the bosom of the people for happiness and life everlasting. The great Spirit told Wovoka that Indians everywhere should dance and have visions in anticipation of His coming once again. They should wear special clothing with sacred designs in order to protect them from the bullets of the white man. Such a Ghost Dance would hasten His coming!

The movement spread like wildfire throughout the prairie West. The Sioux, in particular, embraced it with fervent hope. Sitting Bull went along with it finally as a last hope for his desperate people. White authorities, fearful lest another Indian uprising was in the making, resolved to arrest Sitting Bull and other 'ringleaders' of the movement. On 15th December, 1890, Sitting Bull was shot and killed by police officers sent to arrest him and bring him in. The death of this great Hunkpapa medicine man (the Hunkpapa were a subgroup of the Teton Sioux) resounded throughout the land of the Sioux. One Minneconjou chief named Big Foot, fearful for the lives of his people, fled the reservation with his band. At Wounded Knee Creek they paused to rest and await the imminent coming of the Great Spirit and his cloud. On 29th December, 1890, the revenge-seeking 7th Cavalry massacred 300 of the 350 men, women, and children in Big Foot's band at Wounded Knee, South Dakota. They were mowed down by two Hotchkiss guns mounted on a rise overlooking the Indian camp. The sacred Ghost Dance clothing did not protect these people from the white **103** man's bullets.

Perhaps that mystic warrior of the Sioux people, Black Elk, expressed it best when he said:

'I did not know then how much was ended. When I look back now from this high hill of my old age, I can still see the butchered women and children lying heaped and scattered all along the crooked gulch as plain as when I saw them with eyes still young. And I can see that something else died there in the bloody mud, and was buried in the blizzard. A people's dream died there. It was a beautiful dream . . . The nation's hope is broken and scattered. There is no center any longer, and the sacred tree is dead.'

The Northwest Coast

Stretching from Yakutat Bay in Alaska down the Pacific Coast of British Columbia to the shores of Washington and Oregon is a general cultural region which has been denoted as the Northwest Coast. Here, in a strip of land wedged between coastal mountains and the Pacific Ocean, a people lived and created one of the most remarkable art forms that has ever existed. This is a coastal region of innumerable inlets, bays, coves, and estuaries of important rivers. In the lush forests of this rainy land grow numerous varieties of trees like red and yellow cedar, spruce, fir, pine, and others. Off the mainland coast are innumerable islands ranging from the sizeable Vancouver Island and the Queen Charlotte group to tiny pinpricks hardly worth noting on a map. In sum, it is a land of dense vegetation, rain, fog, and murky atmosphere.

This is the home of the Tlingit, Haida, Tsimshian, Niska, Gitksan, Bella Coola, Bella Bella, Kwakiutl, **1** Nootka, and Salishan tribes. Because the Northwest Coast culture is so complex and varied, most anthropologists have subdivided these tribes into three groups. In the far northern sector—the panhandle of Alaska, the Queen Charlotte Islands, and northern British Columbia—there is the Northern Style of the Tlingit, Haida, Tsimshian, Niska, and Gitksan. In the central sector—the major portion of the British Columbia coastline—there is the Central Style of the Kwakiutl, Bella Coola, Bella Bella, and Nootka (who live on the northwest part of Vancouver Island). And, finally, in the southern sector—the southern portions of British Columbia and the states of Washington and Oregon—there is the very marginal and peripheral culture of the Salishan tribes.

In the Northern Style there is a strong emphasis on two-dimensional painting and carving for surface decoration. In the Central Style, on the other hand, much more stress is given to three-dimensional carving and massive sculptural forms. Insofar as the Salishan peoples had only a minor form of the Northwest Coast culture, we will not consider them further in this book.

The whole Northwest Coast culture was based upon an economy of super-abundance. As anyone might surmise, this was a region where the problem of earning a living was relatively easily solved. The ocean was an exceptionally generous provider of foodstuffs and what it did not offer was easily available in the forests immediately behind the beach. Thus, these people were able to enjoy a varied and balanced diet with the minimum of exertion. In terms of the other means for survival, we can say that here, too, no great

problems were in the offing. Wood and stone were in plentiful supply and the hides of various animals were available to the skilful hunter. Shells for decorative purposes were there simply for the collecting. What this meant was that the struggle for existence was not an all-consuming activity. With the necessities for life taken for granted, these people had the time, energy, and means to develop a complex culture. Their social structure and material goods were probably the most elaborate in North America.

All along the coast people lived in large plank houses constructed from split cedar boards. These houses were big enough to accommodate several families belonging to a clan. Most commonly they would be partitioned into family compartments with the head of the clan and his family enjoying the largest and most commodious of the living arrangements. Often these partitions could be removed during the winter ceremonial period in order to turn the house into a large theatrical arena. The roof was supported by four sturdy interior posts arranged at the four corners of the rectangle. We believe that totem pole carvings might have first made their appearance in the form of carvings upon these house posts. So far as we know, these communal dwellings date back into pre-white antiquity.

With an abundance of raw materials, and wealth as a real possibility, a highly stratified society was created out of differentiated relationships to this wealth. The Northwest Coast was witness to one of the most rigid and meticulously articulated class societies in North America. There were, in fact, four clear class divisions amongst these people. At the top there was the chief of the village and his family of highest nobility. Just beneath them were the aristocracy who enjoyed, like the chief's family, considerable economic wealth, privileges of rank, and other social and material prerogatives. The mass of the village was composed of commoners who lived the everyday life of a free but not privileged people. At the bottom were slaves who were treated as chattels and had no rights as human beings whatsoever.

As Northwest Coast culture evolved, particularly after the period of white contact in the 1770s, there was a distinct tendency to transform all cultural facets into commodities for exclusive and personal possession. That is to say that such phenomena as names, songs, titles, rights to use certain sorts of designs and crests, and the right to claim a particular lineage, became transformed into things that could be owned and used solely by one person and his immediate associates. These things, then, could be bought and

*110. Nakoaktok chief's daughter. When the chief of
Nakoaktok holds a potlach, his eldest daughter is thus
enthroned, supported by statues who represent her slaves.
Photograph by Edward S. Curtis*

sold, won or lost, and handed down from generation to generation. With ownership came the right to claim the exclusive use of that thing; no one else could be permitted to use these commodities without the express and rare permission of the owner. What this meant, of course, was the total 'commoditization' of cultural and social life. It goes without saying that the bulk of these commodities were owned by the nobles and aristocrats since only they could afford them.

Class differentiation in tribal life became so explicit, especially among the Kwakiutl, that each individual knew his particular place within the overall hierarchy. While the four class divisions provided the general form of distinction, every individual within a class knew exactly where he stood in relation to everyone else in that same class. While economic factors were fundamental to the basis of each class, there was a considerable elaboration of power, status, and prestige within each category.

One primary social institution that was associated with this state of affairs was the 'potlatch.' The name derives from a Nootka expression *patshatl* which means 'giving.' A potlatch was a giant social festival hosted by nobles and/or aristocrats within a village in which large quantities of goods would be given away as presents. In the early days the potlatch was a means whereby an important man could establish his claim to own certain types of songs, names, titles, designs, or whatever. He would use the occasion of a potlatch to justify the acquisition of some new honor by lavishly dispensing goods to one and all in his village as well as to guests invited from other villages. A potlatch was commonly used, for example, when a head of a clan might wish to erect a new totem pole to commemorate the distinguished history of that lineage. The capacity of a man to be generous with his possessions was taken as a symbol for his legitimacy to make a particular claim or to take to himself some new items of status.

One side effect of these earlier forms of the potlatch was that it was a convenient way to periodically redistribute the wealth within a village. Since commoners were not in a position to gather luxury commodities, the potlatch was an easy and informal way of seeing to it that goods did not become overly concentrated in the hands of just a few.

Around the middle of the 19th century, however, the potlatch took on new dimensions with such tribes as the Kwakiutl. It became something more than a means to establish claims within a village and to redistribute wealth. The potlatch assumed more competitive and ambitious aspects. The necessity for a man to humiliate and degrade all rivals, real and potential, within his village and outside it, became more pronounced purposes of the ritual. It developed into a 'zero-sum game' in which one man's loss was another man's gain and vice versa. In fact, a man could not claim what he wanted and call the potlatch a success unless he had decimated the pretensions of his rivals. The potlatch emerged as a means for 'fighting with property,' as Helen Codere has termed it (in *Fighting with Property: A Study of Kwakiutl Potlatching and Warfare, 1792–1930*).

In the later, Kwakiutl form of the potlatch, a man would not only invite his friends and neighbors but his rivals and enemies as well. He would distribute gifts, to be sure, but do so in such a manner as to put his rivals at a disadvantage. He might give them a rare and expensive item in order to taunt them with the reminder of his own greater wealth. Or, going further, he might give them a precious object knowing full well that they would have to invite him soon to a potlatch of their own in which they would have to outdo him. Gifts, presented in this manner, became a challenge and a dare to a rival. Could he or could he not go one better than the giftgiver at a later date?

One way in which a man could establish precedence in his status wars with rivals was to exhibit an exaggerated disdain for his own property. He might have valued slaves clubbed to death in the presence of his guests in order to emphasize how great he was and how easily he might replenish such losses. In a frenzy of Dionysian display he might burn rare and precious objects or destroy (or mutilate) valuable coppers symbolizing much wealth. (Coppers were flattened plaques of native-mined and smelted copper with etched designs on them. They were symbols of wealth in the Northwest Coast region and owning one meant that it was worth a great many commodities. For example, one copper could symbolize the ownership of hundreds or thousands of blankets.) Guests before his fire might be amazed to find the flames fueled not with wood but with rare and expensive seal oil. And so it would go. The more reckless and casual a man could be with his wealth, the more prestige he might claim over his rivals.

If the potlatch-giver was successful in his activities, he would have the right to make certain claims that he wished. In addition, he might have the right to sing certain songs or narrate poems at the expense of his rivals. In 1905, the anthropologists Franz Boas and George Hunt recorded this triumphant song of one successful Kwakiutl potlatch-giver:

I am the first of the tribes,
I am the only one of the tribes,
The chiefs of the tribes are only local chiefs.
I am the only one among the tribes.
I search among all the invited chiefs for greatness like mine.
I cannot find one chief among the guests.
They never return feasts,
The orphans, poor people, chiefs of the tribes!
They disgrace themselves.

In 1895, Boas wrote about a Kwakiutl potlatch in which the following exchange took place:

below 114. Carved wooden headdress with killer whale crest. Height 13 in. Tsimshian, British Columbia. Museum of the American Indian, Heye Foundation, New York

bottom 115. Wooden mask representing a mountain hawk. Niska, British Columbia, Canada. Museum of the American Indian, Heye Foundation, New York

opposite 116. Buckskin shirt with brown bear and mountain demon design. Haliotis shell decoration. Length 32 in. Tsimshian, Port Simpson, British Columbia, Canada. Museum of the American Indian, Heye Foundation, New York

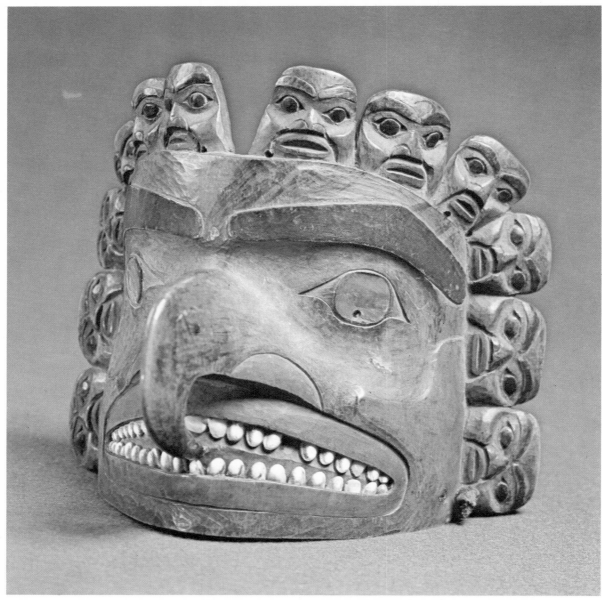

'First Neqapenkem (Ten Fathom Face) let his clan
sing the following song at a feast which he gave:
1. Our great famous chief is known even outside of
our world, oh! he is the highest chief of all. (Then he
sang:) The chiefs of all the tribes are my servants, the
chiefs of all the tribes are my speakers. They are
pieces of copper which I have broken.'

Thus, towards the middle and end of the 19th
century, with the Kwakiutl, the potlatch became a
fabulous ceremony for the display of wealth and the
earning of new ranks of status and prestige.

Other important social events for the Northwest
Coast Indians were their winter ceremonies. In the long
and chilly winter, various secret societies would give
the people an opportunity to witness elaborate dance
dramas. They were not just dances but, in reality,
dramatic ballets and pantomime presentations that
narrated stories of supernatural happenings. The participants would dress themselves in elaborate regalia
and wear stupendously carved masks. Amongst the
Kwakiutl, in particular, these ceremonies reached
exceptional heights.

One of the most interesting of these ceremonials—
one that provides us with some insight into the
Kwakiutl imagination—deals with the Hamatsa Can-
113 nibal Raven drama. In his classic work on the subject,
*The Social Organization and Secret Societies of the
Kwakiutl Indians*, written in 1895, Franz Boas describes
this striking and bizarre ceremonial:

'BaxbakualanuXsiwae . . . initiates several dancers, the
most important of which is the hamatsa, or the
cannibal. He is possessed of the violent desire of
eating men. The novice is taken away by this spirit
and is supposed to stay at his house for a long time.
The period of his absence extends over three or four
months, during which time he actually stays in the
woods. In the middle of his time he reappears near
the village and his sharp whistle and his cries, "hap,
hap, hap" (eating, eating, eating), are heard. Then he
comes back to fetch his kinqalaLala, who must
procure food for him. The kinqalaLala is always one
of his female relatives. Finally he returns and attacks
every one upon whom he can lay his hands. He
bites pieces of flesh out of the arms and chests of the
people. As soon as he arrives, the servants of the
hamatsa, the heliga (healers) or salaLila, of whom the
Kwakiutl have twelve in all, run up to him, swinging
rattles, the sound of which is supposed to pacify the
hamatsa. This office is hereditary in the male line,
and either four or six of them must accompany the
hamatsa whenever he is in an ecstasy. They
surround him in a close circle in order to prevent
him from attacking the people and utter the
pacifying cries "hoip, hoip." The rattles of the heliga
are always carved with a design which originally
represented a skull . . . In olden times, when the
hamatsa was in a state of ecstasy, slaves were killed
for him, whom he devoured. The following facts

were observed by Mr Hunt and Mr Moffat at the
early days of Fort Rupert: When a hamatsa had
returned from the woods, a slave, a man of the
Nanaimo tribe, named Suntem, was shot. They saw
him running down to the beach, where he dropped.
Then all the nuLmal of the Kuexa tribe went down to
the beach carrying knives and lances. The bear
dancers and the hamatsa followed them. The
nuLmal cut the body with their knives and lances
and the hamatsa squatted down dancing and crying
"hap, hap." Then the bear dancers took up the flesh
and, holding it like bears and growling at the same
time, they gave it to the highest hamatsa first and
then to the others. In memory of this event a face
representing BaxbakualanuXsiwae was carved in the
rock on the beach at the place where the slave had
been eaten. The carving is done in sandstone, which
was battered down with stone hammers. Near this
rock carving there are a number of others and much
older ones. The Indians have no recollection of the
incidents which they are to commemorate. They say
that they were made at the time before animals
were transformed into men.'

These astounding people, with their class structure,
potlatches, and winter ceremonies, created a stunning
array of arts. As might be expected, most of the work
attracting our attention is made of wood, sometimes
with abalone shell inlay. Not to be denied, however, are **9**
the textiles of the Chilkat people (a branch of the
Tlingit) who created marvelous blankets and poncho **124**
shirts out of the hair of dogs and mountain goats.

In dating the production of these wonderful arts and
crafts, we are left with the impression that the height
of the Northwest Coast culture was a phenomenon
post-dating the coming of the white man. In other
words, most experts agree that the culture of this
region did not really reach its peak until this contact
was made. While the rudiments or core of the culture
were surely present at the time of white discovery in
1741, it was not until after the fur trade was established
in 1778 that we witness the classic culture of the
Northwest Coast. It is clear that the prime cause of
this development is found in the technology of
Western civilization. The introduction of sophisticated
metal tools made intricate carving feasible. Given pre-
contact aboriginal stone and wooden tools it would
have been impossible to make the masterpieces of
classic Northwest Coast art. The fur trade, however,
introduced a whole galaxy of new tools which the
carvers snatched up in order to perfect and realize
their work. Some indication that the seminal ideas of
this culture were present before Captain Cook sailed
into British Columbia waters is found in his own commentary of 1778:

'They have a truly savage and incongruous
appearance; but this is much heightened when they
assume what may be called their monstrous
decorations. These consist of an endless variety of

below 120. Wooden mask representing a sea monster with the head of a hawk. Kwakiutl, British Columbia, Canada. Museum of the American Indian, Heye Foundation, New York

opposite above 121. Classic wooden mask, painted and decorated with human hair. Tsimshian, British Columbia. Museum of the American Indian, Heye Foundation, New York

opposite below 122. Carved wooden headdress painted to represent the sun. Decorated with human hair. Height 10·5 in. Niska, Nass River, British Columbia. Museum of the American Indian, Heye Foundation, New York

carved wooden masks or visors applied on the face or to the upper part of the head or forehead. Some of these resemble human faces, furnished with hair, beards and eyebrows, others, the heads of birds . . . and many, the heads of land and sea animals, such as wolves, deer and porpoises, and others. But, in general, these representations much exceed the natural size; and they are painted, and often strewed with pieces of the foliaceous mica, which makes them glitter, and serves to augment their enormous deformity . . . It may be concluded, that, if travelers or voyagers, in an ignorant and credulous age, when many unnatural or marvellous things were supposed to exist, had seen a number of people decorated in this manner . . . they would readily have believed . . . that here existed a race of beings, partaking of the nature of man and beast . . .'

Once the new tools were introduced, the arts developed to an unprecedented degree. The actual period of the flowering of this culture can be dated from roughly 1780 to 1890, a span of little more than 100 years. As with the Plains, the classic period of the Northwest Coast was initiated by white contact and came to an end as a result of this same contact. By 1890, the decline and even decay of traditional Northwest Coast life was most pronounced. The ban on the potlatch announced by Sir John A. Macdonald's government in 1885 sounded the death knell for the

continuity of this highly individual way of life.

While it lasted, though, this classic period bequeathed untold art treasures to the world. The totem poles, masks, headdresses, forehead masks, canoes, paddles, Chilkat blankets, potlatch serving bowls, painted ceremonial screens, and the like, continue to impress laymen and connoisseur as the products of a strikingly original imagination.

From all available evidence, we are led to the conclusion that the development of the totem pole was relatively late in this culture. The earliest reports of explorers and fur traders contain no mention of what should have been striking features of a village skyline. It is entirely possible that the Northwest Coast tribes did not conceive of such objects themselves but were introduced to the notion in the early 19th century. One Haida legend states that the idea of a totem pole was first learned when a foreign object was washed up on the shore of one of the Queen Charlotte Islands one day. Another theory suggests that the tribes of British Columbia might have learned the concept from South Pacific seamen who were serving on the fur-trading vessels. There is indeed a remarkable resemblance between totem poles and certain memorial structures found on South Seas islands. Whatever the origins of these heraldic devices, we do know that they were developed most fully and soonest by the Haida.

In reality there was not one but four different kinds of totem poles:

123. Slate carving representing an episode in the legend of the Bear Mother. Here the berry-picker is giving birth to her bear child by Caesarean section; two grizzly bears are assisting her. Height 7 in. Haida, British Columbia, Canada. Museum of the American Indian, Heye Foundation, New York

Memorial poles These are the giant heraldic representations most familiar to the popular imagination. In reality they were family crests and emblems of the owner or his ancestors. At the top was a figure usually thought to be the supernatural ancestor of the particular family or clan. The other figures on the pole symbolized important events in the family history, and usually had to be interpreted by someone familiar with their meaning. Such poles were raised, usually, in memory of some important event and were often celebrated with a potlatch.

Mortuary poles These grave-posts contained the remains of the dead. In order to be honored with such a memorial, one usually had to be a chief, shaman, or person of high rank. Normally the ashes were placed in a box on top of the pole, and this accounts for the reason that most of them had a characteristic front-board (the front-board being the front portion of the box).

House-front poles These were similar to memorial poles except that they invariably stood flush against the front of the plank house. The entrance to the house would be a hollowed-out opening at the lower end of the pole.

House-posts These are amongst the earliest of the totem poles. As an integral part of the house structure itself, they usually served to hold up the roof beams of a plank house. Very often they were four in number and elaborately carved in order to give distinction to the interior of the building.

In order to define the salient characteristics of Northwest Coast art, it is necessary to call attention once again to distinctions between the Central and Northern Styles. The Central tribes, as we noted earlier, developed a preference for sculpture in the round. The two most common objects of Central Style work are totem poles and masks. The Kwakiutl, for instance, produced deeply carved totem poles and painted them with the characteristic colors of black, red, green, and some yellow. Each figure or unit on the pole tends to be a piece of sculpture that could stand on its own, apart from being a section on this heraldic device. Masks of **120** human, animal, and supernatural forms predominate **125** with a very three-dimensional quality about them. However, the Central Style came to be strongly influenced by the Northern Style as time went on. Consequently, towards the late 19th century, the Central tribes began to produce such works as painted ceremonial screens which are very similar to those made further north. Indeed it was the Northern Style that was the source of so many ideas which we have come to associate with Northwest Coast art.

When we allude to Tlingit, Haida, Tsimshian, Niska and Gitksan work, we are speaking primarily of a tradition emphasizing two types of output: painting and **116** the shallow carving decorating totem poles, storage **118** boxes, panels, and other items. While we ought not to exaggerate the differences between the two styles, it

124. Chilkat blanket with killer whale design. Mountain goat hair. Width 71 in. Tlingit, Alaska. Museum of the American Indian, Heye Foundation, New York

is possible to say that for the Northern peoples, carving served primarily to decorate functional articles and not to create three-dimensional representations *per se*. While producing works of less monumental proportions, perhaps, their art is one of incredible finesse and sophistication. The Northern Style is more classical, refined, and aristocratic than its more southerly counterpart. Painting was an important art form from the very beginning amongst the Northern tribes. A highly stylized interpretation of animal and supernatural forms came to predominate here. Designs, emblems, and crests were rendered with a strong sense of line and an imagination marking it as distinctively Northwest Coast. In particular, painting and carving combined in this northern area to produce a style that has not been duplicated anywhere. The six basic characteristics of this style are the following:

1 *Portrayal of things unseen* Realism played almost no part in the art of these people; almost all of their work was non-representational. Figures are encountered that do not and could not exist in real life, although within each tribe there was a common interpretation of each supernatural being. In addition, these painters and carvers often distorted shapes in order to bring out one or other feature that was felt to be of particular significance. Often a kind of X-ray technique was employed whereby the internal structure, as well as the external appearance, of a figure was shown.

2 *Rearrangement of component elements* Certain signs or symbols served to denote each major subject and they became the characteristic mode of portrayal. For example, a beaver was always shown with two large front teeth or a bear might be identified because of his claws and ears. At the same time, however, these component elements might not always been shown in a natural relationship to the other parts of the anatomy. Sometimes all of the parts of a subject might be rearranged for aesthetic or space reasons into a special design. The only way to identify a particular subject was to look for certain tell-tale features. This approach is not unlike Cubism which also broke the natural relationship of anatomical features in order to obtain a new aesthetic. The Northern artists, in fact, were among the pioneers of this concept.

3 *Horror vacui* These artists had an aversion to leaving any space without some form of decoration. Every inch of a surface had to be covered. Sometimes design elements were repeated in blank spaces. A painted screen or Chilkat blanket might contain many eyes, feet, hands, and so on, in order to fill the given space entirely.

4 *Outlining* In the Northern Style each object and its component parts were enclosed by a strong outline. Sometimes the outline was repeated or reinforced by shallow carving.

5 *Sinuous forms* The strong lines of the Northern style were almost never straight. Instead, there was a variety of round, oblong, oval, and circular forms. Ovoids and U-forms, in particular, were very common and often represented such features as eyes, feet, paws, hands, and so on.

6 *Splitting* Since all subjects were primarily an adornment of some functional object, these figures, either painted or in low relief, were fitted to the surface shape of the object. Since most of these wood surfaces were rounded in some way, the subject-matter would be split down the middle and then wrapped around the object. This same principle was also applied when a three-dimensional subject had to be accommodated to a flat surface, like a ceremonial screen. Here, too, the subject would be split and flattened out to be painted or carved upon a flat area.

One of the very interesting art forms of the Haida not yet discussed is their carving in argillite (or slate). Extensive argillite deposits are found on the Queen Charlotte Islands, and hence are in the exclusive domain of the Haida. Argillite is a hard black stone that takes on a beautiful sheen when polished. In the 19th century this form of work became particularly popular for the tourist trade. It began when sailors, on ships involved with the fur trade, sought souvenirs to take back home. Haida carvers soon found they could have a brisk trade in carvings of argillite. While some of the subject-matter was realistic—such as carvings of sea captains and other human figures—the predominant themes were totemic. Haida craftsmen found a ready market for carvings of miniature totem poles, replicas of plank houses, scenes from mythological stories, and so on. Today a few argillite carvings are still available from a select number of artists and they are avidly sought by collectors.

From 1890 to modern times, the culture of the Northwest Coast remained in a grave state of decline. The youth abandoned many of the old ways in order to embrace lower class forms of white culture. In very recent years, partly as a response to white adulation of Northwest Coast art, there has been something of a minor revival. Some British Columbia Indians are giving potlatches once again and skilled artisans are attempting to resurrect the old arts and crafts. Leaders are seeking to recapture some of the traditional community spirit and a few of their efforts are meeting with success. Chief James Sewid of the Alert Bay Kwakiutl has expressed sentiments about a Northwest Coast renaissance:

'Our forefathers had a great philosophy of life and it is under such beliefs and laws that they brought us up. They saw the beauty of nature which surrounded them in all its riches and they tried to capture some of this beauty in their daily lives, in their legends, dances and carvings. My people believed in one Almighty Power who created all things, and they marvelled at and were awe-struck by the grandeur of his creation. Many people have misconceived ideas about our ancestors; it has been thought that they worshipped totem poles or that these were constructed to frighten the enemy! This could not be farther from the truth. Totem poles were memorials; each figure represented a family crest or coat of arms and depicted an episode in the history of the clan. We wish to preserve some of this heritage and all that our architecture, art and dances meant to our people.'
(From S.W.A. Gunn's *Kwakiutl House and Totem Poles*.)

The Woodlands

The Woodlands area in North America is a very large geographical region. It begins in the Yukon River and Mackenzie River systems of Alaska and northwestern Canada and stretches through a whole subarctic terrain. From there it encompasses both the Canadian Shield country north of the Great Lakes and extends south into the fertile lands of the Mississippi and Ohio valleys. Ultimately, it reaches past these inland fresh water systems into the Atlantic region. It also includes the historic Southeastern portion of the United States.

While all the Indians of this territory have in common the fact that they reside in more or less wooded regions, it is not quite fair to the complexity of their cultures to link them all together as one homogeneous unit. Therefore, anthropologists have devised various classifications in order to differentiate these peoples in some meaningful way. One typology that makes both ecological and cultural sense is the following: the subarctic tribes of Alaska and Canada; the eastern Woodlands tribes of the Great Lakes and mid Atlantic region; and, finally, the southeastern tribes of the United States, south of the Ohio valley and east of the Mississippi River. In each of these three regions, the cultures of the various tribes differ according to ecological and economic bases.

In the subarctic lands of Alaska and Canada we find the Athapaskan-speaking tribes like the Hare, Dogrib, Yellowknife, Kutchin, Slave, Chipewyan, and Han. South of the Hudson Bay we can locate the Woodland Cree and northern Ojibway tribes of the Algonkian tongue, as well as the Naskapi and Montagnais. All these peoples depended upon hunting, fishing, and gathering for sustenance. In the main, their diet was composed of caribou, moose, hare, fish, and berries. The struggle for existence was unrelenting and its grim necessities demanded a migratory pattern for all people. In the Mackenzie and Yukon River districts, one or two family units in a tribe might wander about the entire winter in search of food. When summer came, these units would coalesce into bands and camp together near water during the warm weather. With the advent of winter once again, the band would break up into the splintered units of associated families. In the eastern subarctic region the lifestyle was not much different.

The advent of the fur trade did affect the living patterns of these people, however. Apart from the introduction of the white man's alcohol and diseases, these people tailored their existence in order to secure furs for the middleman tribes and/or white fur traders. Founded in 1670, the British-owned Hudson's Bay Fur Company established trading posts all over the Canadian Shield into the subarctic regions. Many tribes came to spend most of the summer encamped near these posts for easy access to trade goods. In the late fall, the family would move into the wilderness where the man might have (in association with relatives) a trap line which he would follow during the winter for the harvesting of furs. As these Athapaskan and Algonkian peoples developed debts with the fur companies, their trapping became a necessity. Each spring the family brought its furs into the post for the purpose of paying back debts and starting the cycle of trade over again. In some of the more remote subarctic regions, this pattern still prevails today although it is being slowly eroded due to increasing contact with the modern white world.

The material culture of this area was simple, functional, and suited to the nomadic existence of the tribes. For transportation in summer they relied upon birchbark and sprucebark canoes. In winter they utilized snowshoes and toboggans. Clothing in winter had to be warm in order to protect the body from sub-zero temperatures; garments made of caribou, moose, and hare hides were decorated with moosehair or porcupine quill embroidery. In the eastern regions, straight and curved lines were painted on clothing in addition to other forms of decoration.

Religion was an important fact of life for these people since existence was difficult and some meaning had to be attached to such an arduous struggle. Theirs was world of spirits and shamans who possessed more power than the ordinary person. Shamans could use their power for good or evil. In the eastern regions, particularly prevalent amongst the Cree and Ojibway, was the ritual known as the 'Shaking Tent.' A shaman would enter a specially built lodge (sometimes he was bound hand and foot) and inside it he would call upon his spirit helpers to answer questions, locate lost articles, and help anyone in trouble. Sometimes the presence of a shaman's spirit helpers was so powerful that the entire tent would shake and vibrate with their actions.

During the course of the winter months, Cree and Ojibway elders would tell legends and stories to the young. At night-time, after the evening meal and around the camp fire, the young would gather to hear a Nakomis (grandmother) tell the old tales about the good and evil spirits of the Algonkian world. In the cosmology of the northern Algonkians, for example, the universe is populated by good and bad supernatural beings. The Great Manitou and Mother Earth, of course, are undeniably beneficent but there are others who lurk in the world to do harm to mankind. Some of the more important figures of legend include:

129. A Cree woman. Photograph by Edward S. Curtis

Wee-Sa-Kay-Jac (supernatural trickster and creator); Windigo (cannibalistic monster of the North); Mishipizhiw (water demi-god who lives in northern lakes); Ja-Ka-Baysh (a figure who risks all challenges regardless of their danger); Guy-An-Way (a mythical god from another world who seeks to destroy cannibalistic creatures); O-Ma-Ma-Ma (earth mother from whom all the spirits come); and many, many more.

Creation legends are particularly interesting since they shed light on the kind of consciousness a people might possess. Below is a Saulteaux (western Ojibway) creation legend told by George Peequaquat of northern Saskatchewan:

'This is a story about Wee-Sa-Kay-Jac we call him. He walks throughout the land. He once destroyed our land long ago. He wasn't too pleased with himself. This earth of ours, flooded, he called the muskrat to dive down to get a piece of earth. So really the muskrat brought some for him. He dried it and blew it. After he blew it they were on an island. The next time he blew it he couldn't see across or how big the island was. And again he blew it, he made a wolf. Then he told him to run around to see how big our land was. He was away for four nights, then he came back, then he said this land of ours would be too small. He blew it again, the earth. Then he sent the wolf off again to run around it. Now he was away for four weeks this time, that wolf. He said the earth was still too small. So again he blew the earth. And he waited. Then finally after fourteen years he got back. He was a very old wolf after fourteen years of running. So this is how big this land will be, that's how he finished.'
(From Nick Johnson, 'Bits of Dough, Twigs of Fire,' Artscanada, December 1973/January 1974.)

Within the last decade, a very important school of native legend painters has come forward in Canada. Their work features strange and striking images which are inspired by the texts of Algonkian myths. The distinguished pioneer painter of this school is an Ojibway from the Sand Point Reserve on Lake Nipigon in Ontario, named Norval Morrisseau. Following his lead, several other artists are actively producing works relating to the subject-matter of traditional legends: Carl Ray, **139** Jackson Beardy, Daphne 'Odjig' Beavon, Joashim **140** Kakegamic, Samuel Ash, and several others. For many Western-orientated viewers, their work may seem incomprehensible and not a little disconcerting. Certainly it is true that no other native painters in North America are producing work comparable to theirs.

Amongst the tribes of the Great Lakes and mid Atlantic region, the struggle for existence was noticeably easier. Their subsistence patterns were also more varied; these tribes, in addition to hunting, fishing, and gathering, would also engage (in varying degrees) in agriculture. Almost all these tribes would grow some kind of crop or crops to supplement their diet; corn, squash and beans being the most common types of produce.

There is an amazing variety of tribes and tribal organization patterns among these people. Some of the more prominent tribes include the Menominee, Saúk and Fox, Winnebago, Ojibway (called Chippewa in the United States), Huron, Shawnee, Miami, Peoria, Illinois, Narraganset, Pequot, Mohegan, Delaware, Powhatan, Iroquois, Susquehanna, and Catawba. The three main linguistic roots of these tribes are Siouan, Algonkian, and Iroquois-Caddoan.

The Iroquois, in particular, are a fascinating people. In reality, the Iroquois are not just one tribe but a confederated nation of six: the Oneida, Onondaga, Mohawk, Seneca, Cayuga, and Tuscarora (after 1715). Legend has it that a Huron refugee named Deganawidah (accompanied by a disciple named Hiawatha) founded the original League of Iroquois Tribes in New York State around 1570. This great shaman and oracle argued that peace and prosperity would be insured if these people would unite with each other instead of staying separate and antagonistic. It is often alleged that the particular formal arrangements of the Iroquois League inspired the founding fathers of the United States in terms of providing them with ideas about federated government and checks-and-balances.

In the Iroquoian political system, women possessed an unusual amount of power. All the male delegates to the ruling councils of the Iroquois nation were designated by senior women in the clan or tribe. These women had not only powers of appointment but recall and impeachment powers as well. Indeed, the whole Iroquois social and political system was based upon the prerogatives of women.

One of the most interesting aspects of Iroquois religious practice is the False Face Society. Believing that sickness is caused by spirits who bring evil with them, the Iroquois seek to overcome or propitiate these evil-doers through dance rituals. Various masks are **130, 138** carved by dancers and used in longhouse ceremonies in order to ward off spirits who cause sickness or to cure those people already afflicted. (A longhouse is the large multi-family dwelling abode of the Iroquois and other semi-sedentary agricultural tribes of the East. During False Face ceremonies, these units are converted into ceremonial chambers.)

In order to participate in such rituals a man would have to dream of a 'False Face' when asleep. He would then go to a living tree and carve a likeness of the face of which he had dreamed. When the face was completely outlined on the trunk of the tree, it was felled and a portion of the log taken home for the finishing of the mask. There were three types of False Face masks. The most important class of mask was that of the spirit-being Shagodyoweh or the Great Doctor who dwelt on the rocky rim of the world. The second class of mask was that of the Doorkeepers who prevented people from entering or leaving a longhouse during a False Face ceremony. And thirdly, there were Common Faces carved in the likeness of beings in the forest who aided the legendary Good Hunter who founded the False Face Society. The first type of mask is often grotesque in form, with strangely distorted facial features. The reason for the grotesqueness of Shagodyoweh is accounted for in the following legend (from E.S. Roger's False Face Society of the Iroquois):

'Now when our Maker was finishing this earth, he went walking around inspecting it and banishing all evil spirits from his premises. . . As the Creator went on his way westward, on the rim of the world

130. False Face mask, wood painted red. Seneca
Iroquois, Allegheny Reservation, New York State. Museum
of the American Indian, Heye Foundation, New York

opposite 131. Beaded shoulder bag. Ojibway. Museum of the American Indian, Heye Foundation, New York

below 132. Beaded shoulder bag. Length 29 in. Creek Museum of the American Indian, Heye Foundation, New York

bottom 133. Quilled birchbark box. Height 4 in. Micmac, Nova Scotia. Museum of the American Indian, Heye Foundation, New York

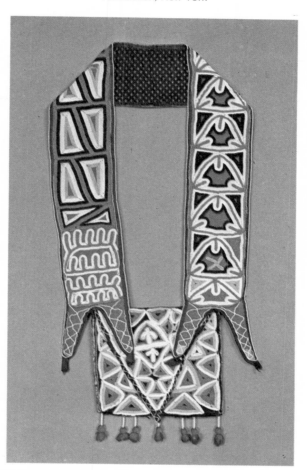

he met a huge fellow– the head man of all the Faces. The Creator asked the stranger, as he had asked the others, whence he came. The stranger replied that he came from the rocky mountains to the west and that he had been living on this earth since he made it. They argued as to whose earth they traversed and agreed to settle the title by contest. The Creator agreed to call the stranger "Headman," should he demonstrate sufficient magic strength to summon a distant mountain toward them. They sat down facing the east with their backs to the west and held their breaths. Now the great False Face shook his giant turtle rattle and the uproar frightened the game animals. He summoned the mountain toward them, but it moved only part way. Now was the Creator's turn, and he summoned the mountain, which came directly up to them. However, his rival, becoming impatient, suddenly looked around, and the mountain struck his face. The impact broke his nose bridge, and pain distorted his mouth . . . Now the Creator realized that this fellow had great power. He assigned him the task of driving disease from the earth and assisting the people who were about to travel to and from hunting. The loser agreed that if humans make portrait masks of him, call him grandfather, make tobacco offerings, and set down a kettle of mush that they too shall have the power to cure disease by blowing hot ashes. The Creator gave him a place to dwell in the rocky hills to the west near the rim of the earth, and he agreed to come in whichever direction the people summoned him.'

The Iroquois originally lived in what is now upper New York State and resided in more or less permanent settlements. They constructed sturdy longhouses out of poles and bark which could accommodate several families at once. Adjacent to their pallisaded villages were fields of corn, squash, beans, and tobacco. The women were primarily responsible for raising the crops while men saw to hunting, fishing, and the protection of the village. Insofar as they tended to have a more sedentary existence than most, their arts and crafts included such articles as pottery.

Iroquoian pottery, like most Eastern pottery, is made in a different way from the ceramics of the prehistoric Southwest. Whereas the latter were made by the coil technique, the Iroquois and others used modeling and paddling techniques. With these methods, clay is laid over the bottom of an inverted jar (which serves as a mold), and the clay is spread over this mold with a paddle. The paddle ensures the fact that the clay is spread evenly and thinly over about a third of the curved mold. The bowl is then shaped after it has been separated from the mold. Sometimes a clay anvil or anvil stone was used in order to proceed with the shaping of the bowl. The paddle would be used opposite an anvil in order to extend the sides of the bowl and thin and smooth them out. If a deep bowl or water jar was being made, coils might be added to the upper portion of the bowl in order to build it further. **142** Then the bowl might be decorated with incised designs. While the Iroquois preferred incising, other Eastern tribes employed impressing, engraving, and stamping techniques. Whatever the particular variation, Eastern pottery is quite distinct from that of the Southwest, although quite impressive in its own right.

The Huron, Tobacco, and Neutral nations of the Ontario area had a similar social structure to the Iroquois of New York. The Huron and Iroquois clashed, however, in the era of the fur trade over who was to be pre-eminent as middleman between the tribes of the interior and the white trading firms. The Hurons tended to align with the French while the Iroquois were usually on the side of the British. Therefore, their tribal warfare had more at stake than merely the middleman question; it involved the contest of two great European mercantile nations as to which was to exploit the riches of the New World. The contest between the Huron and Iroquois was settled when, in 1649, the Iroquois launched a devastating raid against the Hurons which crushed them as a power. From that time on, in a general sense, the Iroquois were the dominant middlemen of the Hudson River area for the receiving and transferal of furs. To the north however, the Ojibway and Cree were contracted by Hudson's Bay Company as middlemen in the Canadian Shield region.

The patterns of subsistence and social life were considerably varied in this region as a whole, however. Not all of the tribes were sedentary agriculturists like the Iroquois and Huron. The Ottawa and Potawatomi were semi-agriculturists but they relied considerably on game, fish, and wild fruits to supplement their diet. During the winter these two tribes, like the Ojibway, would break up into smaller units for hunting purposes. In these more compact family groups they would hunt bear, beaver, elk, deer, muskrat, and other animals. In spring and summer the tribe would reconstitute itself and establish common villages on lakes where they would do a bit of farming and gathering.

The Winnebago and Menominee of Wisconsin pursued a pattern of existence which differs from the Ottawa and Potawatomi. These two tribes lived in permanent villages and maintained fields of corn, beans, squash, and tobacco. The Menominee depended heavily on harvesting wild rice in the fall, while the Winnebago went out on the prairies in the fall for a communal buffalo hunt. The Sauk and Fox and Miami tribes also hunted buffalo on the prairie, doing so primarily in the fall and winter.

The Ojibway were perhaps more nomadic than most of their near neighbors. Like their subarctic relatives, they tended to live in portable dwellings which were dome-shaped and covered with birchbark. These lodges were termed 'wigwams.' In the fall the Ojibway would harvest wild rice and in the spring they would gather maple syrup. During the winter they would break up into family units for hunting purposes, and in the summer they would re-establish the village. In the springtime they would plant corn in fields, and then abandon it to nature until the harvest in the fall. Theirs was a culture that bore a greater resemblance than most to the subarctic modes of existence further to the north in the Shield.

The Ojibway, amongst other tribes of the Upper Great Lakes, were involved with a religious ritual society known as the Midewiwin. The Society was formed in order to help cure the sick. Both men and women could join. The Society had eight grades or orders of membership: the four at the top were known as the Sky Midewiwin and the four at the bottom were known as the Earth Midewiwin. In the initiation rites for this society, medicine bundles with special powers were

134. Cornhusk mask. Seneca Iroquois, Cattaraugus
Reservation, New York. Museum of the American Indian,
Heye Foundation, New York

152

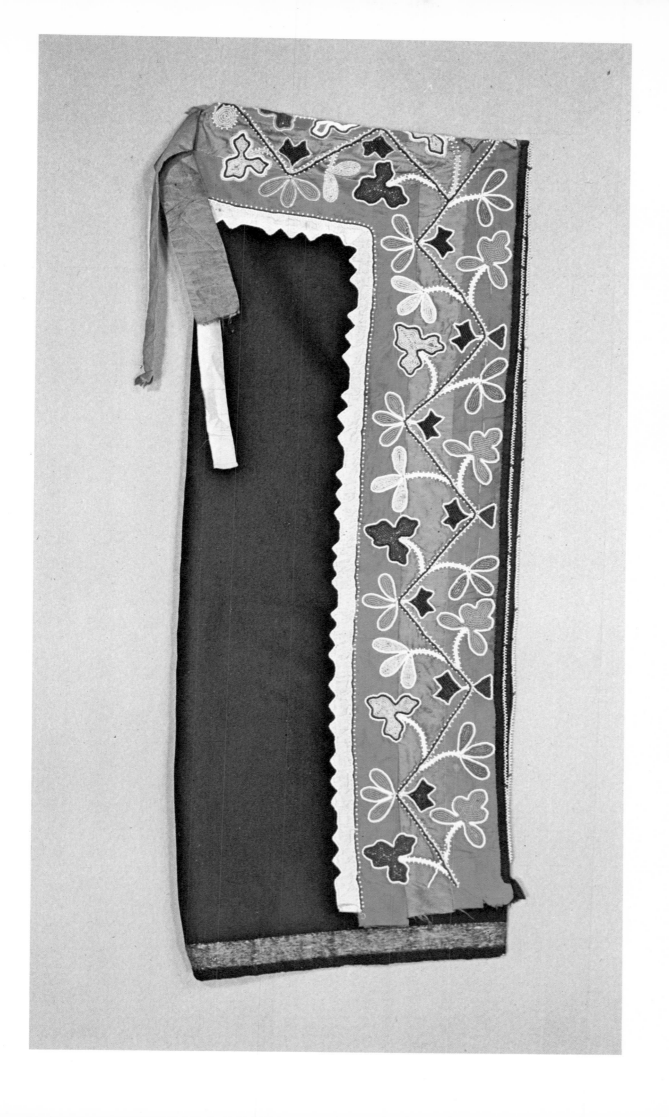

used in order that the power of one bundle could be 'shot' (directed) into other participants. Birchbark scrolls existed with sacred symbols, pictures, and mnemonic devices for each of the eight levels of the Midewiwin. Any owner of one at an appropriate level could interpret the scroll in order to understand the significance of that order of the Society. The Midewiwin was an important society since the world was full of malevolent and evil-doing spirits which had to be confronted or counteracted by an opposing power. Power was an important concept for those people since one had to possess at least minimal amounts of it in order to carry on existence and survive. Shamans with power of good and evil were an important feature of life, and their existence could not be ignored by anyone. The Midewiwin Society served as an institutional force whereby members could hope to obtain some power for themselves in order to have security and protection from the malevolent spirits of the universe.

One of the most important crafts amongst these tribes was the embroidery and decoration of tanned hide articles of clothing. At first, most embroidery incorporated quillwork. As G. Stuart Hedge has commented:

'In the Great Lakes area quillwork was outstanding. An examination of its various techniques, and refinement in color and design is very rewarding. To fashion a brilliant craft from the defensive armor of a most uprepossessing creature is ingenious and imaginative in itself.'

With the advent of the fur trade and the introduction of beads, bright colored glass cylinders began to take their place alongside quills, and even to replace them altogether. Together with such technical innovations came new ideas in design. One of the most important influences was the naturalistic art of the white man. Before the white man, we think, their designs, even when of a floral nature, tended to be simple abstractions and symbols. After the introduction of white ideas, however, the designs took on greater realism. Floral beadwork, for example, became quite lifelike and very elaborate.

Items like shoulder bags demonstrate how the introduction of beadwork and new ideas in design motifs caused new developments. While there are those who believe that shoulder bags date back to aboriginal times, a more plausible explanation is found in the notion of white contact. Eastern Indians must have seen many bandoleer bags of French and British soldiers and been impressed by the elaborateness of these functional cartridge-belt holders. Using their imagination, they abandoned the functional aspect of these bags and transformed them into part of their ceremonial
6 equipment. These shoulder bags were now heavily
131, 132 beaded, usually, with either the spot-stitch sewing or loomwork techniques. The visual effects are extremely beautiful.

In addition to beadwork and quillwork, ribbonwork
10 was another form of craft employed in the eastern
133 Woodlands. Birchbark and wood materials also became

the basis for pleasingly decorated utensils and containers. In Minnesota, there was the great Catlinite quarry where all tribes could come in peace and obtain the beautiful red stone for the manufacture of pipes. **136** And finally, the finger-weaving of sashes and the production of yarn bags reached real pinnacles of excellence in the 19th century.

In the Southeast, a Woodlands culture continued unbroken from prehistoric times. While it is true that the Mississippian culture was already in significant decline when Spanish explorers visited the region, the living culture of the Southeast, just like that of the Southwest, bore an organic relationship to its ancestors. The Natchez of the lower Mississippi still bore a striking resemblance to the Moundbuilders of the true Mississippian culture of previous times. Under the pressure of colonization by Spanish and French peoples, however, these older tribal traditions were destroyed.

In fact, the remaining Indian tribes of the Southeast had lost most of their 'Indian-ness' by the early part of the 19th century. Five tribes in particular became so acclimatized to white norms and values that they were known as 'The Five Civilized Tribes': Choctaws, Cherokees, Chickasaws, Creeks, and Seminoles. Their adoption of white manners and customs did not save them from the greed of the white man, though. In the 1820s and 1830s these tribes were forced to remove themselves from their ancestral lands and take up residence in the 'Indian territory' of Oklahoma. The forced removal of these people to an alien and incompatible environment is one of the most tragic chapters in a book of sorrows on white relations with the Indians. Forcibly uprooted from their native soil, these people suffered untold hardships in the exodus to Oklahoma. Some, like the Seminoles, fought long and hard to preserve their tribal lands, but in the end most were removed as ordered by Washington, DC. Only a few remain in the Southeast as testimony to traditions that once went back centuries.

Oklahoma was selected by federal authorities as a dumping ground for many eastern Woodlands tribes. Here, in this southern Plains state, a Tower of Babel existed as many tribes from the Woodlands and northern Plains were settled with indigenous peoples in the one area.

The relentless march of the white man has destroyed most of the original Indian cultures of the Woodlands region. Only in the subarctic areas of Alaska and Canada and in the Canadian Shield do we still find inhabitants with a more or less distinctive Indian lifestyle; and even this is melting away quickly in the second half of the 20th century. The white man's passion for land and his greed and covetousness for the riches of eastern North America caused him to desolate the native life of that region. While the weight of white presence is felt everywhere, in many areas of the east in the United States it is impossible to locate any tribal cultures still living and viable. The Iroquois of New York State and Ontario have done better than most in preserving their culture from total annihilation. For most Americans on the Atlantic seaboard, nonetheless, the Woodlands cultures of that region are nothing but a historical memory.

left 138. False Face 'Harvest' mask, wood decorated with cornhusks and horsehair. About 1870. Onondaga Iroquois, New York State. Museum of the American Indian, Heye Foundation, New York

opposite above 139. **Legendary Bear**, *by Joashim Kakegamic. Acrylic paint on illustration board. Woodlands Cree. Sandy Lake Reserve, Ontario, Canada*

opposite below 140. **Wee-Sa-Kay-Jac and the Magic Mishipizhiw**, *by Samuel Ash. Acrylic paint on illustration board. Ojibway. Lake St Joseph Reserve, Ontario, Canada*

below 141. *Pipe tomahawk. Length 20·75 in. Iroquois. Museum of the American Indian, Heye Foundation, New York*

bottom 142. *Pottery jar with human figure in relief. Incised brown ware. Height 8·75 in. Iroquois, Madison County (Beechard site), New York. Museum of the American Indian, Heye Foundation, New York*

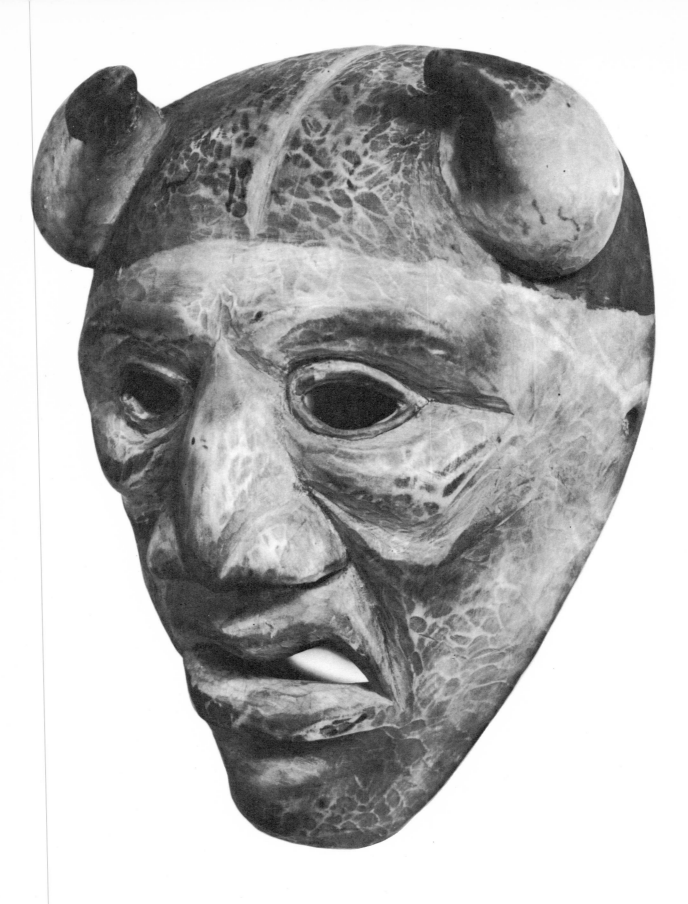

above 143. Wooden buffalo mask used in the Booger Dance. Cherokee. Museum of the American Indian, Heye Foundation, New York

opposite above 144. Tomahawk pipe. Eastern Woodlands. British Museum, London

opposite below 145. The Chippewa Snow-shoe Dance by George Catlin. This dance was performed to thank the Great Spirit for sending the first snow of winter, for thick snow made it easier for the hunters to chase the game on their snow-shoes. British Museum, London

159

California and the Far West

In our narrative on the life and art of the North American Indian, we have not dealt extensively with three cultural areas: the Plateau, Great Basin, and California.

In terms of the Plateau region, we have selected some aspects of that culture and discussed them within the context of the Great Plains development. The Plateau region shares many traits in common with the Great Plains since physical and cultural contact between the two was pronounced. The Plateau cultural area itself is mainly a hybrid one. It borrowed heavily from both the Great Plains and Northwest Coast, although much more from the former. Many of its largest and most prominent tribes—the Nez Percé, Flathead, Kutenai, Kalispel, Coeur D'Alene, Umatilla, Cayuse, and others—crossed over the mountains into the Plains regularly in order to hunt buffalo. Furthermore, they obtained the horse even earlier than most of the Plains tribes and became equestrian hunters and raiders much like them. As a hybrid development, the Plateau culture was heavily affected by acculturation to white values, and what remains today is oriented towards the Plains.

As regards the Great Basin and California areas, they have been combined in the present chapter. The reason for this is not because their cultures are identical but because their major contribution to arts and crafts is generically similar: baskets. Both the California and Great Basin peoples excelled in the manufacture of beautiful and durable baskets.

The peoples of the Great Basin region were mainly Shoshonean-speaking tribes. Some of the more prominent tribal groups in the region include the Paiute, Ute, Washo, Modoc, Klamath, Bannock, Gosiute, and Shoshone proper. The Great Basin encompasses the modern states of Nevada, Utah, and parts of Wyoming and Oregon. These people lived a very simple existence of gathering with a little hunting to supplement a vegetarian diet. They practised no agriculture whatsoever. Since the region is one of extensive deserts and a warm climate, the basic social unit was the nomadic extended family. The resources of the region simply did not permit much in the way of more extensive social groupings. Although their material culture was oriented to a subsistence-level economy, they did produce some baskets of exceptional excellence.

California is the home of more than 100 tribes speaking numerous dialects of six different language stocks. In the northwest part of the state are the Yurok, Wiyot, and Hupa who are fairly similar to the Northwest Coast tribes. Many of the tribes in the eastern part of the state are very similar to the Great Basin peoples like the Shasta, Yana, Maidu, Wintun, Miwok, and Yokuts. Along the southern California coast are the easy-living Indians like the Salinan and Chumash. The abundance of food resources in the state and the mild climate permitted these native peoples an easy mode of living. Consequently, the material culture was never under any pressure to develop. Many tribes, nonetheless, produced baskets which are second to none.

The Pomo in the northern part of the state became particularly famed for the production of superlative coiled and twined baskets. Their globular gift baskets **149** are extraordinary in quality and often decorated with shell beads, spotted with the feathers of quail or wood- **14** pecker, or completely decorated with feather mosaics. The Karok to the north of the Pomo also made baskets utilizing the quills of birds for decorative purposes. The baskets of these people have to be seen to be fully appreciated.

White culture has been particularly destructive to the fragile cultures of these simple people. In California, as early as 1769, the Spanish were establishing missions that were to divorce many tribes from their traditions. The Gold Rush of 1848 was an unmitigated disaster for California's Indians, and their cultures have never recovered from the blows dealt by greedy and rapacious miners. In today's world, for most of the tribes in the California and Great Basin region, their past is but a distant memory as they live in poverty amidst an indifferent white population.

146 *Gathering tules, Lake Pomo. Tules (bulrushes) were used for thatching houses, making mats and in the construction of canoes. Photograph by Edward S. Curtis*

opposite above 147. A Pomo woman weaving a latticed
twine basket. American Museum of Natural History,
New York

opposite below 148. Basket with human figure design,
decorated with feathers and shell beads on the rim. Height
6 in. Pomo, California. Museum of the American Indian,
Heye Foundation, New York

below 149. Globular basket and cover. Height 9 in. Chumash,
Santa Ynez, California. Museum of the American Indian,
Heye Foundation, New York

bottom 150. Basket made by Datsolali. Height 4·75 in. Washo,
Carson City, Nevada. Museum of the American Indian,
Heye Foundation, New York

163

Acknowledgments

The publishers are grateful to the following for the illustrations reproduced in this book:

Courtesy of the American Museum of Natural History; The Author's Collection; British Museum; Carmelo Guadagno; The late Edward S. Curtis; Glenbow-Alberta Institute, Calgary, Alberta; Courtesy of Museum of the American Indian, Heye Foundation; Rare Book Division, The New York Public Library (Astor, Lenox and Tilden Foundations); Shostal Associates Inc.; U.S. Department of the Interior, National Park Service.

Author's acknowledgments

As is a truism by now, any author like myself accumulates an immense debt with regard to friends, colleagues, and students. A book such as this could not have been written if it were not for these associations, past and present.

Turning to traders and dealers whom I have known over the years, I would like to acknowledge: Paul and Kay Huldermann of the House of Six Directions in Scottsdale, Arizona; Cliff and Mae Fleming of Flagstaff, Arizona; Byron Hunter, Jr, of Scottsdale, Arizona; Don K. Price of Albuquerque, New Mexico; Mary Williams of the Museum of the American Indian, Heye Foundation, New York City; Norma Reincke of New York City; Tom Woodard of Gallup, New Mexico; the Tanner family of Gallup, New Mexico; Walter J. Crawford of Phoenix, Arizona; Norma Bird of Fort Qu'Appelle, Saskatchewan; James Luongo of Monroe, New York; the late Tom Bahti of Tucson, Arizona; the late Mrs Wilson of Palm Springs, California; and the late H. T. Daniels of Fontana, California.

In terms of my Indian friends, I would like to acknowledge: Joe and Alice Carrier of the Piapot Reserve, Saskatchewan; Bella Nahnepowish of the Piapot Reserve, Saskatchewan; Bernadette Atcheynum of the Sweetgrass Reserve, Saskatchewan; Violet Four Horns of Regina, Saskatchewan; Maria Shepherd of Regina, Saskatchewan; Wayne Goodwill of the Standing Buffalo Reserve, Saskatchewan; Stella Goodwill of the Standing Buffalo Reserve, Saskatchewan; Henry and Teresa Beaudry of the Mosquito/Grizzly Bear's Head Reserve, Saskatchewan; Clarence Swimmer of the Sweetgrass Reserve, Saskatchewan; Chester and Daphne 'Odjig' Beavon of Winnipeg, Manitoba; Jackson Beardy of Winnipeg, Manitoba; Wm. Guy Spittal of Ohsweken, Ontario; Dorothy Francis of Vancouver, British Columbia; Richard Ironchild of Regina, Saskatchewan; Caroline Bonaise of the Little Pine Reserve, Saskatchewan; Michael Lonechild of the White Bear Reserve, Saskatchewan; Sanford Fisher of the Gordon's Reserve, Saskatchewan; John and Mary Louise Rockthunder of Regina, Saskatchewan; and Harry Nicotine of the Chitek Lake Reserve, Saskatchewan.

To my closest friends, there is no measurement of my indebtedness and they will know who they are.

My thanks also go to my colleagues in the Departments of Sociology, Political Science, and Anthropology at the University of Regina. My gratitude to all my students, past and present, reminds me of Seneca's observation that 'A teacher by his students is taught.'

A special word of thanks must go to my editor at Hamlyn's, Deborah Trenerry,because working with her on the project has been a pleasure from the beginning.

John Anson Warner
Regina, Saskatchewan, Canada
13th August, 1974

Bibliography

This is a very selective bibliography of works pertaining to the life and art of the North American Indian, past and present. No effort has been made to be comprehensive. Instead, these are a few titles that the author feels to be useful for further study.

Adair, John, *The Navajo and Pueblo Silversmiths*, University of Oklahoma Press, Norman, 1944

Amsden, Charles, *Navajo Weaving*, Fine Arts Press, Santa Ana, California, 1934

Appleton, L. H., *Indian Art of the Americas*, Charles Scribner's Sons, New York, 1950

Barbeau, Marius, *Totem Poles*, 2 vols, Bulletin No. 119, Anthropological Series No. 30, National Museum of Canada, Ottawa, 1930

Barbeau Marius, *Haida Carvers in Argillite*, Bulletin No. 139, National Museum of Canada, Ottawa, 1957

Barbeau Marius, *Indian Days on the Western Prairies*, Bulletin No. 163, National Museum of Canada, Ottawa, 1960

Boas, Franz, *Primitive Art*, Dover Publications, New York, 1956

Brody, J. J., *Indian Painters and White Patrons*, University of New Mexico Press, Albuquerque, 1971

Colton, H. S., *Hopi Kachina Dolls*, University of New Mexico Press, Albuquerque, 1959

Covarrubias, Miguel, *The Eagle, the Jaguar, and the Serpent*, Alfred A. Knopf, New York, 1954

Davis, Robert Tyler, *Native Arts of the Pacific Northwest*, Stanford University Press, Palo Alto, California, 1949

Dockstader, Frederick J., *The Katchina and the White Man*, Cranbrook Institute of Science, Bulletin No. 35, 1954

Dockstader, Frederick J., *Indian Art in America*, New York Graphic Society, Greenwich, Connecticut, 1961

Dockstader, Frederick J., *Indian Art of the Americas*, Museum of the American Indian, New York, 1973

Douglas, Frederic H. and René d'Harnoncourt, *Indian Art of the United States*, Museum of Modern Art, New York, 1941

Driver, Harold E., *Indians of North America*, University of Chicago Press, Chicago 1961

Drucker, Philip, *Indians of the Northwest Coast*, AMS Press Inc., New York, 1963

Dunn, Dorothy, *American Indian Paintings of the Southwest and Plains Area*, Albuquerque, 1971

Ewers, John C., *Blackfeet Crafts*, Haskell Institute Press, Lawrence, Kansas, 1945

Ewers, John C., *Plains Indian Painting*, Stanford University Press, Palo Alto, California, 1939

Feder, Norman, *American Indian Art*, Harry Abrams, New York, 1971

Feder, Norman, *Two Hundred Years of North American Indian Art*, Whitney Museum of American Art, New York, 1971

Goddard, P. E., *Indians of the Southwest*, American Museum of Natural History, New York, 1931

Gunther, Erna, *Art in the Life of the Northwest Coast Indians*, catalogue of the Rasmussen Collection at the Portland Art Museum, Seattle, 1966

Haberland, Wolfgang, *The Art of North America*, Crown Publishers Inc., New York, 1964

Hawthorn, Audrey, *Art of the Kwakiutl Indians*, University of Washington Press, Seattle, 1967

Hodge, Frederick W., *Handbook of American Indians North of Mexico*, Bulletin No. 30, Bureau of American Ethnology, Washington, 1912

Holm, Bill, *Northwest Coast Indian Art*, University of Washington Press, Seattle, 1965

Inverarity, Robert Bruce, *Art of the Northwest Coast Indians*, University of California Press, Berkeley, 1950

Jennes, Diamond, *The Indians of Canada*, Bulletin No. 65, National Museum of Canada, Ottawa, 1932

Josephy, Alvin M., Jr., *The Indian Heritage of America*, Alfred A. Knopf, New York, 1968; Jonathan Cape Limited, London, 1972

La Farge, Oliver, *A Pictorial History of the American Indian*, Spring Books, London, 1962

Lowie, Robert H., *Indians of the Plains*, McGraw-Hill Book Company, New York, 1954

Lyford, Carrie A., *Iroquois Crafts*, Haskell Institute Press, Lawrence, Kansas, 1945

Lyford, Carrie A., *Ojibwa Crafts*, Haskell Institute Press, Lawrence, Kansas, 1945

Lyford, Carrie A., *Quill and Beadwork of the Western Sioux*, Haskell Institute Press, Lawrence, Kansas, 1940

Miles, Charles, *Indian and Eskimo Artifacts of North America*, Henry Regnery Company, Chicago, 1963

Mochon, Marion Johnson, *Masks of the Northwest Coast*, Publications in Primitive Art, No. 2, Milwaukee Public Museum, Milwaukee, 1966

Masterpieces of Indian and Eskimo Art from Canada, Société des Amis du Musée de l'Homme, Paris, 1969

Patterson, Nancy Lou, *Canadian Native Art*, Collier-Macmillan of Canada, Ltd., Toronto, 1973

Ritzenthaler, Robert, *Iroquois False-Face Masks*, Publications in Primitive Art, No. 3, Milwaukee Public Museum, Milwaukee, 1969

Siebert, Erna and Werner Forman, *North American Indian Art*, Paul Hamlyn, London, 1967

Sloan, John and Oliver La Farge, *Introduction to American Indian Art*, catalogue for the Exposition of Indian Tribal Arts, New York, 1931

Stirling, Matthew, *Indians of the Americas*, National Geographic Society, Washington, D.C., 1955

Swanton, J. R., *The Indian Tribes of North America*, Bulletin 145, Bureau of American Ethnology, Washington, D.C., 1952

Tanner, Clara Lee, *Southwest Indian Craft Arts*, University of Arizona Press, Tucson, 1968

Tanner, Clara Lee, *Southwest Indian Painting, A Changing Art*, University of Arizona Press, Tucson, 1973

Underhill, Ruth, *Pueblo Crafts*, Haskell Institute Press, Lawrence, Kansas, 1944

Underhill, Ruth, *Red Man's America*, University of Chicago Press, Chicago, 1953

Underhill, Ruth, *The Navajos*, University of Oklahoma Press, Norman, 1958

Vaillant, George C., *Indian Arts in North America*, Harper & Bros, New York, 1939

Wardwell, Allen, *Yakutat South: Indian Art of the Northwest Coast*, Art Institute of Chicago, Chicago, 1964

Waters, Frank, *The Man Who Killed the Deer*, The Swallow Press, Chicago, Illinois and Neville Spearman, London, 1942

Waters, Frank, *Masked Gods: Navaho and Pueblo Ceremonialism*, Swallow Press, Chicago, Illinois, 1950

Waters, Frank, *The Book of Hopi*, Viking Press, New York, 1963

Waters, Frank, *Pumpkin Seed Point*, Swallow Press, Chicago, Illinois, 1969

Whiteford, Andrew Hunter, *North American Indian Arts*, Golden Press, New York, 1970

Willey, Gordon R., *An Introduction to American Archaeology, Vol. I: North and Middle America*, Prentice-Hall, Inc., Englewood Cliffs, New Jersey, 1966

Wissler, Clark, *The American Indian*, Oxford University Press, New York, 1938

Wissler, Clark, *Indians of the United States*, Doubleday & Co. Inc., New York, 1940

Wormington, Hannah M., *Prehistoric Indians of the Southwest*, Denver Museum of Natural History, Popular Series, No. 7, 3rd edition, Denver Museum of Natural History, Denver, 1956

The following books and articles have been quoted in the text:

Benedict, Ruth, *Patterns of Culture*, Houghton Mifflin Company, Boston, 1934; Routledge & Kegan Paul, London, 1935

Boas, Franz, *The Social Organization and Secret Societies of the Kwakiutl Indians*, 1895. Reprinted by the Johnson Reprint Corporation, New York, 1970

Josephy, Alvin M., *The Indian Heritage of America*, Johnathan Cape Limited, London 1972

Matthews, Washington, *Navajo Legends*, American Folklore Society, Philadelphia, 1897

Rogers, E. S., *The False Face Society of the Iroquois*, Royal Ontario Museum of Toronto, Ontario

Waters, Frank, *The Man Who Killed the Deer*, Swallow Press Inc., Chicago, and Neville Spearman, London, 1942

Index

The figures in bold refer to illustrations

167

Iroquois 150
Lino black-on-gray 41
Lino gray 41
Mancos black-on-white 35, 41
Mesa Verde black-on-white 45
Mimbres black-on-white **19**, **27**, **28**
Pecos polychrome 45
Picuris 77
Reserve black-on-white 41
Sagi black-on-white 45
St John's polychrome 45, **25**
San Ildefonso 77, **57**
San Juan 77
Santa Clara 77
Sikyatki polychrome 45, 84
Taos 77
Tularosa black-on-white 45
White Mound black-on-white 41
Zia 77
Zuni 45, 77, **62**, **63**
Powhatan tribe 146
Problem of Indian Administration, The by Lewis Meriam etc 16
Pueblo Bonito 39, 41
Pueblo Revolt (1680) 50, 52, 73, 95
Pueblo tribe 21, 25, 35, 38, 50, 52, 53, 73–84
Keresan-speaking 73
Shoshonean-speaking 73
Tanoan-speaking 73
Zunian-speaking 73
Pumpkin Seed Point by Frank Waters 11

Queen Charlotte Islands 122, 138, 143
Quetzalcoatl 31
Quillwork 20–21, 25, 118–121, 144, 155, **11**, **87**, **94**, **102**, **133**
Quintana, Ben 88

Radiocarbon dating 28, 31
Rain-in-the-Face 92
Rainy Chief **109**
Ray, Carl 146
Red Cloud 92
Reservations 16, 21, 53, 60, 61, 92, 118, 121
Rhoads, Charles J. 16
Ribbonwork 155, **10**
Rio Grande 45, 50, 73
Roberts, Frank H. H. 38
Roberts typology 38
Roger, E. S. 146
Roman Catholic Church 21, 50
Roosevelt, Franklin D. 16
Roscoe White Eagle 118
Rouse, Irving 38
Roybal, Alfonso 84

St John's 45
Salado culture 37–38
Salinan tribe 160
Salishan tribe 122
San Carlos 53
Sanchez, Abel 84
Sanchez, Desideria 77
Sandia 73
Sandia Man 32
Sandpainting 61, 64–72, **53**
San Felipe 73
San Francisco mountains 84
San Ildefonso 21, 23, 73, 77, 84, **57**
San Juan 73, 77
San Juan river 38, 39
San Lorenzo *see* Picuris
San Pedro Cochise 32, 35
Sans Arc tribe 92
Santa Ana 73
Santa Clara 21, 73, 77
Santa Fe 16, 50, 84, 85, 88
Indian School 85, 88, 118
Institute for American Indian Arts 88
Museum of New Mexico 85
School of American Research 85
Santayana 77
Santee Sioux tribe 92
Santo Domingo 73
Sapp, Allen 118
Saskatchewan 118
Saskatchewan river 95
Sauk & Fox tribe 146, 150, **11**
Saulteaux tribe 146
Secret societies 130
Seminole tribe 155
Seneca tribe 146, **130**, **134**
Separate Reality, A: Further Conversations with Don Juan by Carlos Castaneda 6
'Seven Cities of Cibola' 50
Sewid, James 143
Shaffer, Owen Vernon 24
'Shaking Tent' ritual 144
Shamans 144, 155, **4**
Shasta tribe 160
Shawnee tribe 146
Shellwork 25, 37, 41, 49, **14**, **16**, **32**, **33**
Sheridan, Philip 121
Shipaulovi 73
Shiprock 61
Shoshone tribe 160
Shungopovi 73
Siberia 28
Sichomovi 73, 77
Sihasapa tribe 92
Sikyatki 84
Sinagua culture 37
Sings *see* Chants
Sioux tribe 12, 25, 90, 92, 95, 107, 118, 121, **4**, **85**
Sipapu 41
Sisseton tribe 92
Sitting Bull 92, 107, 118, 121
Skinwork 25
Slate carving **123**
Slave tribe 144
Sloan, John 16, 84
Social Organization and Secret Societies of the Kwakiutl Indians by Franz Boas 130
Sonora 31, 38
Soto, Ferdinando de 45, 49
Southern Cult 49
Southern Death Cult 49
South Sea Islands 138
Southwest Indian Craft Arts by Clara Lee Tanner 77
Spanish conquest 50–52, 53
Spirit Quest 107–110
Spiro Mound 49, **33**, **38**
Spruce Tree House 41, **23**
Stonework 25, **38**, **39**
'Storm pattern' 61
Stylization 17, 35
Sulphur Springs Cochise 32
Sun Point Pueblo 41
Susquehanna tribe 146
Symbolism 17, 35

Tafoya, Margaret 77, **57**
Tafoya, Serafine 77
Tahoma, Quincy 88
Tanner, Clara Lee 77
Taos 73, 77
Teachings of Don Juan, The: A Yaqui Way of Knowledge by Carlos Castaneda 6
Tea-drinkers Society **79**
Teec Nos Pos 61, **48**
Tesuque 73
Teton Sioux tribe 92, **87**
Textiles 25, 53, 61, 130, **45**, **48**, **49**
Tezcatlipoca 31
Tierra del Fuego 28
Tiger, Jerome **107**
Time 16
Tipis 25, **87**
Tlaloc 45
Tlingit tribe 122, 130, 139, **15**, **118**, **124**
Tobacco tribe 150
Toke, Monroe Tsa 110
Toledo, Jose Rey 88
Toltecs 31
Tomahawk pipe **141**, **144**
Tonto 41
Tonto Basin 37
Toreva 73
Totem poles 20, 138, 139, 143
house-front 139, **128**
house-posts 139
memorial 139
mortuary 139
Trading 60, 61, 102
fur 20, 21, 90–92, 121, 130, 138, 143, 144, 150, 155
Travois **105**
Tsimshian tribe 122, 139, **114**, **116**, **121**
Tsinajinnie, Andy 88
Tsireh, Awa 84
Tuba City 61
Tuscarora tribe 146
Tuzigoot 41
Two Gray Hills 23, 61
200 Years of North American Indian Art (exhibition) 16, 17
Two Kettles tribe 92

Umatilla tribe 121, 160
Utah 31, 38, 160
Ute tribe 160

Vancouver Island 122
Velarde, Pablita 88
Vigil, Romando 84
Vlahos, Olivia 23
Wahpekute tribe 92
Wahpeton tribe 92
Wallace, Lincoln **118**
Walnut Canyon 41
Walpi 73, 77, **68**, **72**
Walpi tribe 84
Washington, D.C. 31
Washington State 122
Washo tribe, 160, **150**
Waters, Frank 11–12, 177
Weaving 25, 53
Crystal 61
Ganado 61
Navajo 53, 60–61
Shiprock 61
Teec Nos Pos 61, **48**
Tuba City 61
Two Gray Hills 61
Wide Ruins Trading Post 61, **49**
See also Textiles
Wee-Sa-Kay-Jac 146
Wee-Sa-Kay-Jac and the Magic Mishipizhiw **140**
White Eagle 118
Whiteford, Andrew Hunter 24
White Mountain 53
Whitney Museum of American Art *see* New York
Wichita tribe 90
Wide Ruins Trading Post 61, **49**
Wigwams 48, 150
Windigo 146
Winnebago tribe 146, 150
Wintun tribe 160
Wisconsin 49, 150
Wisconsin ice sheet 28, 47
Wiyot tribe 160
Woodwork 25, 130, **9**, **15**, **41**, **112**, **114**, **115**, **118**, **120**, **121**, **122**, **126**, **127**, **138**, **143**
Wool 53
Wounded Knee 12, 21, 121
Wovoka 121
Wupatki 41
Wyoming 118, 160

Yana tribe 160
Yanktonai Sioux tribe 92
Yankton tribe 92, **82**
Yarok tribe 25
Yeheh-gouhu **117**
Yei design 61
Yellowknife tribe 144
Yesterday They Rode **107**
Yokut tribe 160
Young-Man-Afraid-of-his-Horses 92
Yukon river 144
Yuma tribe 84, **70**
Yurok tribe 160

Zia 73, 77
Zuni Corn Dance **74**
Zuni Pueblo 45, 50, 73, 77, 84, **58**
Zuni tribe 61, 73, 76, 84, **54**, **62**, **63**, **74**